one

SINGLE MOTHERING
FULL CIRCLE

karen sjoblom

Barb —
Thank you for
everything on this
long journey!
Ka

Scripture quotations in this publication are taken from the Holy Bible,
translations as follows:
VOICE: Scripture taken from The Voice™. Copyright ©2008 by Ecclesia Bible
Society. Used by permission. All rights reserved.
NIV: Scripture quotations marked (NIV) are taken from the Holy Bible,
New International Version®, NIV®. Copyright © 1973, 1978, 1984, 2011
by Biblica, Inc.™ Used by permission of Zondervan. All rights reserved
worldwide. www.zondervan.com The "NIV" and "New International Version"
are trademarks registered in the United States Patent and Trademark
Office by Biblica, Inc.™
GW: GOD'S WORD is a copyrighted work of God's Word to the Nations.
Quotations are used by permission. Copyright 1995 by God's Word to the
Nations. All rights reserved.
NLT: Scripture quotations marked (NLT) are taken from the Holy Bible,
New Living Translation, copyright © 1996, 2004, 2007 by Tyndale House
Foundation. Used by permission of Tyndale House Publishers, Inc., Carol
Stream, Illinois 60188. All rights reserved.
NASB: Scripture quotations taken from the New American Standard Bible®,
Copyright © 1960, 1962, 1963, 1968, 1971, 1972, 1973, 1975, 1977, 1995 by
The Lockman Foundation. Used by permission. (www.Lockman.org)
ESV: Scripture quotations marked (ESV) are from The Holy Bible, English
Standard Version® (ESV®), copyright © 2001 by Crossway, a publishing
ministry of Good News Publishers. Used by permission. All rights reserved.
MSG: Scripture taken from The Message. Copyright © 1993, 1994, 1995,
1996, 2000, 2001, 2002. Used by permission of NavPress Publishing Group.

Library of Congress Control Number: 2016904401
ISBN 13: 978-1530791705
ISBN 10: 1530791707

Cover design and layout by Machele Brasss, www.brassdesign.net.

Printed in the United States of America.

Dedicated to
Cathy Brewer
&
the remarkable women
of Eve's Daughters.

This wouldn't have been possible
without you.

contents

foreword   ix

1) one deep breath   1

The Hardest Part   2
Starving   4
Peace in the Midst   6
Keeping It Real   8
Prodigal's Rest   10
For Giving   12
Cat with an Uzi   14
Seek the Pony   16
Imagining Disaster   18
Enough Already   20

2) one part letting go   23

Taking Flight   24
Sorry   26
Listen Up   28
Day Five   30
Let Go of the Rope   32
Death and Life   34
Shifting Gears   36
Wishing Well   38
Wistmastime is Here   40
Heart of Stone   42

3) one dose of reality   45

Strong Enough to Cry   46
Vaguely Familiar   48
Risky Business   50
The Sisterhood of the Traveling Brain   52
Easy Does It   54
The Amazing Invisible Woman   56
Mystery Mom   58
Weakness Wins   60
A Different Kind of Good   62
Waiting in the Dark   64

4) one good cry   67

The Cleansing   68
Good Byes   70
Today   72
Fatherless But Fathered   74
Exploring the Depths   76
All That's Sacred   78
One Less   80
Small Comfort   82
Giving Up   84
Halved in the Sharing   86

5) one different angle   89

Girly Man   90
Life in the Meantime   92
The Gift of Right Now   94
Do You See What I See?   96
Thanksgiving   98
Exiting Chaos   100
The Grateful Place   102
Running on Empty   104
Silencing the Voice   106
Last August   108

6) **one mustard seed**   111
   Signposts   112
   On Faith   114
   Trust Me   116
   Bounty   118
   Going Out   120
   The Desires of Your Heart   122
   Shameless   124
   Good Service   126
   Building Altars   128
   Everything in Season   130

7) **one faithful tribe**   133
   Give a Little Bit   134
   Showing How It's Done   136
   Joining Hands   138
   Where We Left Off   140
   Who Do You Think You Are?   142
   Glorious Rentals   144
   Come Together   146
   You Are Here   148
   Lighting the Way   150
   Less-Than   152

8) **one dab of tenacity**   155
   What Will They Remember?   156
   Things No One Ever Told Me   158
   The Business of Reality   160
   The Tiny Life   162
   But What About Me?   164
   The Weight of Being an Anchor   166
   Beyond the Cape   168
   Showing Up   170
   Latch on to the Affirmative   172
   What Does Your Saturday Look Like?   174

9) **one more chance** 177

The Gifts of Pain 178
Lost and Found 180
Pick Your Poison 182
One Generation Removed 184
Getting Into Alignment 186
Putting the Pieces Together 188
Feeling It 190
Worst Foot Forward 192
Redemption 194
For a Little While 196

10) **one moment of hope** 201

Great Expectations 200
Scatter Joy 202
All Things New 204
Peace Out 206
And One More Thing… 208
Realistic Hope 210
Grace and Peace 212
Ancient Beauty 214
Joy in the Morning 216
The End of This Journey 218

afterword: one hard goodbye 221

acknowledgements 223

**on building your own
single mom community** 224

foreword

There came a shift during late elementary school when my daughter decided more is better. More friends. More attention. More doodads. More colors. Choices. Options. Chocolates. *More.*

In the years since, we've had many discussions about how lucky we are to have one good friend—someone who builds up instead of tears down, who listens, who's trustworthy, who's got our back. Maybe even one more than we deserve.

Years ago, when I was going through a really hard time, I asked a very wise person in my life how in the world I would make it through. He said *one.*

One afternoon with a friend
One phone call
One Kleenex passed
One black laugh
One timely hug

As single moms, we've got a lot going on and, usually, we ourselves fall to the bottom of the list. But the old adage is not only true, but wise: If you're going to pour into someone else, best to dip from a well that actually has water in it. My hope is that these short stories, along with friends, family, and God, will help fill you up regularly.

One is a compilation of writings for Eve's Daughters, which was a small, faith-based non-profit in Portland, Oregon, that operated from 2007 until 2016. My business partner, co-founder, and friend Cathy Brewer and I started it as a way to connect single moms to each other, to local resources, to parenting tools and emergency funding and, most importantly, to faith and hope. Cathy was about five years down the road from me with regard to her own divorce, and I came to see how lucky I was to have her in my life. She was one of my *one*s who walked me through the shaky first years of single parenting. We recognized not everyone was so fortunate and wanted to do something about it, thus Eve's Daughters was born, offering a place of community—our own little family.

I write to encourage single moms through all our common emotions—the exhaustion, fear, wonder, and grief, for sure—but also the unexpected joy, pride, and, ultimately, hope that arise as we learn we can actually do this gig. Far from a "how-to" manual, the essays here are meant to meet you where you're at, so you can read a story or two, put the book down, and come back another time for more hope, more understanding. Rather than chronologically, these stories are arranged topically and span the phases single moms seem to go through. There may be times you need to change your vantage point, so you'll read the "One Different Angle" section from start to finish. In other seasons, you may be crawling through the seemingly never-ending pit of grief, and need to camp out in the "One Good Cry" chapter for a while to remember you will indeed make it out.

Maybe you've experienced Eve's Daughters or something like it firsthand. If not, I wish for you your own funny, supportive tribe of single moms who get it, and get you, and will walk with you on the long journey to get your babies raised in community. After 15 years of doing this on my own, I know: It can feel as though you're the only woman who's ever had to slog through this…but my hope is that something on the following pages will offer you a little taste of encouragement when you need it most.

Just one.

1

one deep breath

ON FACING YOUR FEARS,
FINDING THE TRUTH, AND
TRYING SOMETHING NEW

the hardest part

Some days it feels the whole of my single mom life has been spent waiting and hoping for dark to give way to light. All those years ago it was a hard, hard realization that I, too, brought much to the divorce party—that it wasn't all his fault, and that life wasn't suddenly perfect when he was gone. I brought all my crap with me to my new home with a then three-year-old daughter to raise, and let me just say—it was crowded. But finally, when all I had left was the tenacious desire for my daughter to not repeat my life, I came back to God, paid professionals, and laypeople with a yearning to be healed and a willingness to wait for it.

What I didn't know was, even all these millions of hours of counseling and recovery meetings later, I'd still be waiting: For what I want, for what I don't have, for what I may never have. Like a four-year-old trying to stay awake on Christmas Eve, it's the waiting I find the hardest.

Years ago, I was at a church service that featured people holding cards over their heads during a song. One card front read, "Motherless." Then, the card was flipped: "Adopted baby girl 2006." Throughout the procession, the solutions seemed so *immediate*, but having walked alongside most of the card-flippers I know they slogged many dry miles before getting their answers. Many times their original dreams had to die before a different one could take place, and God knows those dreams were often pried from their hands, covered in claw marks.

In my work with Eve's Daughters, I hear a lot about waiting and about dreams dying. It's part of the gig and, frankly, part of my life as well. But I'm starting to believe it's not an anomaly, but rather that we *live* in a period of Advent, a season of waiting, regardless of the calendar. Within each of us, all the time, something is coming into being—a new and different life. No doubt most of us would gladly return to the old and safe at times, but something is definitely stirring if we peer deep: new jobs, new nests, new friends, new callings, new dreams.

The truth is, we cannot stay where we're at and, for a lot of us, this is good news.

For those of us waiting—on jobs and money, on wayward children and hope to go on—it seems interminable, the dark and cold unyielding; how easy to forget something's happening below the surface. In community, though, what a gift it is to learn we no longer have to wait alone for life to stir again.

How did you survive the crises that seemed like they never would end?

What could you teach your children about your own lessons on waiting in life?

ONE VERSE FOR THOUGHT:
Yet I am confident I will see the Lord's goodness while I am here in the land of the living. Wait patiently for the Lord. Be brave and courageous. Yes, wait patiently for the Lord.
–Psalm 27:13-14, NLT

starving

Many years ago at Safeway, I retrieved a fresh gallon of milk from the back of the cooler, turned to place it in my cart, and noticed a gaping hole in the top of my open purse. My wallet was gone. Stunned, I turned around, searching, and noticed a slight man walking away from me quickly, toward the outside doors. He appeared from behind to be lifting his shirt and tucking something in his waistband.

"Hey!" I called, like an idiot—like he was going to turn around and talk to me. But he did...and the discussion got crazier as I asked for my wallet back, promising not to call security. Finally, he tossed it toward me and motioned awkwardly with his arms, like he was totally beaten down, and cried, "Lady, I'm *hungry!*" I couldn't get my thoughts together fast enough to make a difference as he ran out of the store. My too-late call for him to please wait so I could buy him some groceries just hung in the air, along with the irony of saying that while standing in a supermarket stacked to the rafters with food.

Maybe you have felt a similar way—starving from loneliness while surrounded by people, thirsting for your family's support while being met with judgment, or hungering for deeper connection at a church more comfortable with keeping it shallow. What you desperately want and need is right there in front of you, but you can't quite get your arms around it.

I've thought about this man often over the years. In a sense, all he needed was right there in front of him. He didn't have the means *per se*, but the means could have come, via community...maybe even from a woman who needed just a couple extra moments to get her bearings. There could have been lots of people willing to help him that day, at Safeway and elsewhere, and God only knows what could have happened out of any of those encounters.

How often are we starving, in and around each other? Know this much is true: People are willing to feed us with the nourishment of community if we can be brave enough to talk about our hunger and muster the tiniest bit of willingness to come to the table.

Which areas of your life leave you hungry for more connection?

How do you cope with the loneliness of being a single parent, or of simply being human?

ONE VERSE FOR THOUGHT:
Blessed are the poor in spirit,
    for theirs is the kingdom of heaven.
Blessed are those who mourn,
    for they will be comforted.
Blessed are the meek,
    for they will inherit the earth.
Blessed are those who hunger and thirst for righteousness,
    for they will be filled. **–Matthew 5:3-6, NIV**

peace in the midst

In the beginning of my divorce proceedings, when I knew I was doing the right thing but the extrication process was going to be brutal, I would take Emma, then twenty-two months old, to the Oregon coast so she could play in the sand and I could just breathe. There is something about the scent of water and fish, sand and foam, that cleanses my soul like nothing else. But there's also nothing like viewing the ocean to feel your insignificance so deeply, and that is what I felt at the time: so small, so fragile. So easily replaced.

Amidst the heartbreak and anger, many threats were made toward me as to whether I would get to continue being Em's mom, a job I'd been doing pretty well for the previous couple of years. In those days, I feared: for myself, for Emma, for an unknown future. I feared for money, for health, for sanity. I feared for the hole in my girl where her parents used to be, and for the bigger one that would have developed had I stayed. It was as constant as the tides, that fear, and I got very well-practiced at bracing myself for it, as well as the subsequent waves of grief.

There was no peace. I was not free.

But somehow by the water, my fears ebbed. Despite the vastness of the ocean, there was something or Someone there I believed would carry me, not allowing me to drown in an unknown future but buoying me for some purpose I could not yet see. I had just barely come back to God and did not know what I know now—all the promises and provisions that have taken place—but the water has beckoned me back over the years. It's where I feel Him most.

This becomes my solace every time the fear threatens to overtake—when I wonder where and how my girl will land, when I worry about having to work until I'm ninety, when I grieve over not having the large, supportive, intact family for which I ache. He calls me, and reminds me, and promises me the peace I cannot fathom. And finally, I am free.

Where do you go to find peace?

How do you manage the fears you may have about your future?

ONE VERSE FOR THOUGHT:
The Lord is my shepherd, I lack nothing. He makes me lie down in green pastures, he leads me beside quiet waters, he refreshes my soul. **–Psalm 23:1-3, NIV**

keeping it real

One of my favorite Eve's Daughters' events is our annual Spa Night—a child-free time when moms get spoiled with massages, haircuts, makeovers and gift cards and we get to laugh and laugh at our kids' expense. Every year I ask our moms to write out something funny that happened while parenting, and I read the stories aloud as we distribute the gift cards. From instances of kids projectile-puking on store cashiers to sending Junior to see whether Grandpa is still breathing, our moms are adept at finding the black humor in childrearing.

One woman with two truly lovely teenagers shared that, when they were younger, her kids were being so unruly she sat them down and told them she'd just called their biological mother to come and get them. She was *done*. The entire room erupted in howling laughter because, of course, we've all been there.

I shared that my daughter's third year (which of course coincided with the divorce) was absolutely hideous. Once I brought her into a larger bathroom stall in the children's wing at church and, while I was sitting on the toilet, she just decided it was time for her to leave...so she opened the latch and walked out. I was left at the far end of a stall with my pants around my ankles, and the equivalent of a barn door flapping in the wind three feet from my grasp while curious children peered in at me. Good times.

But perhaps the most beautiful part of this sharing is the practically audible release of fear—the thoughts of whether only *our* children are particularly awful, whether *we* are terrible mothers. We gasp in our laughter as we bask in a community of struggle and question, learning once again that so many of our fears are unfounded and our children will indeed be fit to roam the earth soon enough, despite the instances that nearly drive us to drink.

Of all the assignments I've had in life, none has worn down my rough edges faster than being a parent. But if we can keep it real in our community, we'll get what we need to do another day, with more laughter and less fear. When we don't have the answers, someone else likely does; when we need comfort or validation, someone can provide it. And when all hope is lost, we can share the stories that let us know we're not anywhere near alone.

Which instances stand out as times you feared for your kids' futures in a humorous way?

How do you find support and solidarity when you're worried about your children's behaviors or choices?

ONE VERSE FOR THOUGHT:
Finally, brothers and sisters, keep rejoicing and repair whatever is broken. Encourage each other, think as one, and live at peace; and God, the Author of love and peace, will remain with you. **–2 Corinthians 13:11, VOICE**

prodigal's rest

My friend Cathy bought me a spoon rest for my kitchen that reads, literally, *Rest.* It was a gift to go with my word-themed kitchen plaques as well as a tongue-in-cheek reference to something neither of us does terribly well.

Somehow, I've turned rest into a four-letter word. I am a Type A. It's in my genes, passed down from a thousand generations of strong, overachieving, farm-stock women. I am a runner, so to speak (though, sadly, I do not have the runner's body to show for it). It's my false belief I can keep chaos, loneliness, guilt, shame or boredom at bay by moving quickly.

But deep down, we know: Running takes us places we don't want to go. Slowing our pace and coming back to center, even when it's humbling, provide the place of perfect rest. I don't know why I repeatedly need to get lost and burnt out in activity before I realize how much I need to slow down and get restored. I see when it happens, like an accident in slow-motion: the irritation with my daughter, the frustration with my clients, the dark under-eye circles down to about my chin. As single parents, we can feel pulled in myriad directions simultaneously, but those frayed ends tend to let go at the most inopportune times.

My daughter is, I think, a Type Z. Like, *Zzzz.* On weekends, she reads, naps, knits, sings, draws and takes care of her soul. She putters. I race around like a cyclone, trying to catch up. When I putter, it's incredibly restorative: Why don't I do that more often?

Let's give ourselves the gift of getting centered, asking what we're running from and what we're running to, and how a much-needed time-out can change our perspective of the two.

Say yes to rest.

What prevents you from giving yourself rest?

How might life be different if you scheduled it in regularly?

ONE VERSE FOR THOUGHT:
Remember the day of rest by observing it as a holy day. You have six days to do all your work. The seventh day is the day of rest—a holy day dedicated to the Lord your God...
–Exodus 20:8-10, GW

for giving

A guest pastor once said something to the effect that we may be the only Bible others are reading, referring to the fact that we're supposed to be, you know, actually *living* our faith in the world. I hadn't been to church in a long time, but I felt compelled to go that day, and that pastor may as well have thrown a Bible upside my head. How often do I forget that people watch and listen to me when I'm snarky, complaining, cussing, or despondent? Do I come across as hopeless...or hope-filled? As victim or redeemed? Compounding this issue is the need for us to be reconciled to whomever or whatever in order to be authentic, transparent, real. And sadly, this involves the often painful experience of forgiving.

This last year has, frankly, been tough. There's been a lot of loss—of people, relationships, and support. I've been adrift, questioning and feeling pretty lonely and forgotten. But if I take the pastor's words to heart, then I need to take steps to make things right with people if I want my parenting, my writing, and my work with Eve's Daughters to have the scent of authenticity to it, versus the stink of withholding, of unforgiveness, of bitter disappointment.

Through a long, clumsy process, I've learned people who've hurt us often don't deserve our forgiveness, but we deserve to be people who forgive—that we are made *for giving*—but some days I forget. I'm at that critical crossroads yet again: forgive and make progress, or don't and stay stuck.

My desire to be right, to be vindicated, fights with my desire to be free. But for now, I'm trying to be "willing to be willing"—to loosen my fist a bit, to relax into a softer ending and live my life with imperfect grace. And I know if I stay willing, forgiveness will come with silent steps when I least expect it—when I suddenly find I'm no longer in this tight-fisted place, when the scenery suddenly opens up with wide, hopeful spaces.

How strong is the fight to be right in your life?

What have you given up—both good and bad—when you've forgiven someone who doesn't really deserve it?

ONE VERSE FOR THOUGHT:
Then Peter came to Jesus and asked, "Lord, how many times shall I forgive my brother or sister who sins against me? Up to seven times?" Jesus answered, "I tell you, not seven times, but seventy-seven times." **–Matthew 18:21-22, NIV**

cat with an uzi

When Em and I moved into our townhouse, it hit me harder than I'd have expected that I was entirely responsible for her well-being. I would not have considered myself a fearful person, before that move; I'd lived alone and taken care of myself just fine for many years. But throw a tender three-year-old into the mix and, well, I got a little nuts. Were the doors locked, the oven off, the kitchen knives far back enough on the counter? And the night noises: I know women stop sleeping soundly when they have children, but every house creak had me bolting upright at full attention.

One night, I heard a loud thump on the deck, adjacent to and below my room. I caught my breath and listened as my heart pounded. My deck is surrounded on all sides by house, garage and dividing walls; someone must have come over the roof! *And he probably has an Uzi!!* I waited, every muscle twitching, for the inevitable door-crushing-glass-busting-bad-guy-entrance.

Nothing.

The next night, there was another loud thump and, again, I rose like an arthritic ninja with my pitiful Goodwill baseball bat that I keep next to my bed, painfully aware it was no match for a submachine gun. I made my way downstairs in the darkness, my mind playing out all kinds of scenes…until I saw my neighbor's cat, whom I affectionately referred to as Fat Harold because he weighed about forty-seven pounds, lolling about on my patio furniture. He was just making his evening rounds over the dividing wall and glared at me for disturbing his rest.

Em and I can laugh at this now, but the absolute terror I had early on was almost debilitating. Given my history, it made no sense that I was paralyzed with fear for not having an adult male in the house, but I recognized it as just another layer in the transitioning process. It took slowly but surely coming back to God and getting into community to realize I really wasn't alone, other moms could totally relate to my panic and, above all, we were being watched over by eyes that never sleep.

In the years since, I've woken to the sounds of water dripping through light fixtures, humans and animals crying (or, even better, puking), neighbors dying, and far more…and I haven't had to deal with one single Uzi. Yet.

What fears have come to the surface since you've been a single mom?

Who do you rely on to keep those fears at bay?

ONE VERSE FOR THOUGHT:
I look up to the mountains—does my help come from there? My help comes from the Lord, who made heaven and earth! He will not let you stumble; the one who watches over you will not slumber. Indeed, he who watches over Israel never slumbers or sleeps. **–Psalm 121:1-4, NLT**

seek the pony

In recent years, one of my nieces commented that I didn't seem to get nearly as worked up about life as she did, and wondered how that came to be. I told her that happens right after the thing you can't possibly survive occurs... when you learn you'll survive anyway. I know she didn't really know what I was talking about yet. And I know she will eventually, because life is like that. I mostly hope she'll remember the part about surviving.

While I'd categorize myself as a fatalist with a good sense of humor, I have become uncharacteristically amenable to screwing up. I'm a recovering perfectionist, so this didn't come easily. But like the old joke about wading through manure with the belief there must be a pony somewhere, there's something incredibly optimistic and freeing about moving forward with abandon when you know what you've already endured.

So many of our Eve's Daughters moms have found themselves left with multiple kids, a low-paying job (or the non-paying job of mommy-in-arms), and a mortgage they can't afford, with a soon-to-be-ex-partner who's found someone new and isn't terribly interested in supporting the first round of kids. *Try surviving **this***, life seems to say. But these same women, who come to us utterly terrified, pale and shaking, figure out a way to go back to school so they don't have to constantly worry about money. They connect with and support other single moms so they don't have to raise their kids alone. They make their way through the resentment and surface after the potentially paralyzing aftershocks of a separation and decide to forgive and clear the debris, if only on their side of the street. They get to the point of being able to say, "My relationship didn't make it, but we will."

Once that can happen—when we can equate "failure" to a time-bound event, not the whole of who we are—all bets are off. Then we may start our own businesses, write our own books, celebrate our kids' awards, get out of debt, invest in our futures, fall in love, trust again, and so much more.

We need to celebrate our losses, if only because they propel us into a whole new realm of possibility. God will pave the way to make it through, no matter what. Just keep your eyes out for that pony.

What is one of your big dreams—despite all your current obstacles?

In what ways could you help it become a reality?

ONE VERSE FOR THOUGHT:
Since you are precious and honored in my sight, and because I love you, I will give people in exchange for you, nations in exchange for your life. **–Isaiah 43:4, NIV**

imagining disaster

I read a great story once about a woman being "prevent-ed" from worrying; that is, she was instructed to acknowl-edge fear as her first, primary choice, and then ask herself, "What is my second choice?" After doing this exercise for a week, she came to a startling conclusion: The fears that were incapacitating her were actually the fears of those in her family. She'd absentmindedly collected them, like coins on the street, and applied them to her own life, regardless of whether they were true.

After reading and thinking about that piece, I realized I have a deep fear of snakes because my mother has a deep fear of snakes…even though I personally have not had a bad experience with one. I learned I come by my worry naturally, from a long line of women who were black-belt loin-girders: If there was a tornado, Depression, famine, rabid dog, or poisonous wombat in a thousand-mile radius, they were pre-pared. Of course these things never came to pass, but let's not quibble about that; the point is, they worried in advance and were ready. Just in case.

I've lived the bulk of my life in just-in-case mode and all it's really done is suck the joy out of the day. I've worried about running out of money, being unable to work, falling ill, my daughter being kidnapped (or worse), none of which has come even remotely close to happening. Even more comical, now when I meet people who live like this—those who won't eat at salad bars or buffets because others may have germed up the food, for example—my first reaction is, *Lighten up, al-ready!* (If God wants to take me out because I went to a des-sert bar, so be it. There are worse ways to die.)

But, oy—when the worry spills onto our children, and *they* start to become worriers, we've got to pull ourselves together. The world is indeed a scary place, but how much worse do we make it by imagining fresh new disaster lurking around every corner?

You'll start to see it, as I did with my own girl early on: the tiny furrowed brow, the pulling back, the hesitation. That's when we've got to take a deep breath and give them a little shove between the shoulder blades, calming our own fears as we help them move forward and bolster their confidence. Yes, there's plenty of disaster in life to go around...but it's up to us to give our kids the tools to pass through the rough spots and enjoy the scenery whenever possible.

Which worries have spilled over onto your kids?

What would life look like if you were able to let go of your fears and enjoy what's in front of you?

ONE VERSE FOR THOUGHT:
Can all your worries add a single moment to your life?
–Luke 12:25, NLT

enough already

I had another awesome opportunity recently to hear some-one's opinion of me. If I had a nickel for every time this happened, I would be lounging in my Italian villa by now. Over the years, depending on the circumstances, I've been too smart, too stupid, too tall, too serious, too snarky, too Jesusy, too fat, too judgmental, too depressed. Overall, *too much*. Or, conversely, not thin enough, not happy enough, not bright enough, not mature enough, not lighthearted enough, not Christian enough, not loveable enough. Just in general, *not enough*.

As you might imagine, such sentiments can make a girl feel all special inside. But I keep coming back to the bottom line—am I too much, or not enough? For years, I just want-ed someone to please tell me so I could get my act together and do things right. But in my slightly wiser senescence, I'm learning I actually may be enough already.

Maybe you have felt the same labeling your whole life. Maybe it increased in volume and intensity when you be-came a single parent. Maybe others thought you needed to try harder, or you had too many expectations. Maybe they believed you asked too much, or your love wasn't strong enough. Perhaps they believed sharing these opinions with you would change your life. How thoughtful of them! But we learn as parents that labeling our kids backfires; instead of better behavior, our *too much*es and *not enough*s only help us stunt them, blame them, shame them and lose them. Why would it be any different for us? They're not the only ones who suffer under labels: We ourselves lose a lot—self-esteem, motivation, hope—and we're never too old to feel the sting.

Were you always called flaky and unreliable? Controlling and quick-tempered? Cold and isolating? Hard-hearted and driven? Focus especially on pronouncements from former spouses, bitter boyfriends, and those who feel unfulfilled in their lives: Is there *any* truth from which you can learn, grow and change? If not, maybe those labels should be tossed in the garbage permanently for some new titles you'd like for yourself: *nurturing, protective, encouraging, quirky, dedicated, witty, wise, lasting.*

Not just *enough*, but *more than*.

Under which labels have you chafed your whole life?

In what ways are you more than enough already?

ONE VERSE FOR THOUGHT
The Eternal will finish what He started in me. Your faithful love, O Eternal One, lasts forever; do not give up on what Your hands have made. **–Psalm 138:8, VOICE**

2

one part letting go

ON DEALING WITH LOSS, LEARNING TO FORGIVE, AND SOFTENING OUR HEARTS

taking flight

Some of the deepest learning that happens in our house is when we're poking fun at each other. Our church offered a four-week Parenting Teens class that began on my birthday. In talking with my daughter about delaying celebrations and the overall time commitment, she very sweetly said, "Mom, you don't need a class. You're a great parent."

Motioning to my watch, I said, "But you're supposed to get 'ugly' here pretty soon, telling me you hate me and I'm ruining your life. If I go to the class, I'll know how to deal with it."

She rolled her eyes. We bantered some more. In the end, she wanted me to stay home.

And in the end, I registered for the class. Why? Someone a lot wiser than I reminded me that her job these days is to separate from me. And sometimes that means removing myself from her, literally, to make the process a little easier.

Single parents and their kids can become excruciatingly close, which can be both remarkably lovely and ridiculously claustrophobic. How do we nudge them toward independence and the feelings of success that brings them if we're hanging onto their ankles? How do we "have a life" and prepare for an empty nest if they're hanging onto ours?

My daughter now flies alone to the east coast to see her dad, but the first trip was a *real* trip. Despite my fear (and after about twenty-seven hours of travel pointers), I put my baby bird on a plane and hoped for the best. Apparently, it was so uneventful as to be mundane.

As she continues to grow and mature, I'm learning this is life at its most bittersweet—for them to let us go, for us to facilitate it, and for all of us to return to each other, changed.

Which instances in recent years have required you to let go of your children?

Was it more difficult for you, or them?

ONE VERSE FOR THOUGHT:
Start children off on the way they should go, and even when they are old they will not turn from it. **–Proverbs 22:6, NIV**

sorry

It's five-dollar Friday at Safeway and I send my girl in with
a bill for a roasted chicken. A few minutes later I get a text:
It's actually seven. Can you bring in more money? I find her at the
deli, somewhere between surprise and embarrassment, as
the gentleman behind her paid the extra two dollars, and
he's long gone.

Now, I'm the one embarrassed, thinking *for-the-love-of-
God-I-can-afford-an-extra-two-bucks-but-it's-FIVE-dollar-Friday.* I
made a joke that backfired, making it seem she was inept; as
soon as it left my mouth, it made a beeline for my sensitive
girl's heart. I apologized. She forgave even before she knew
what she was doing, reassuring me, "It's alright, Mom."
Sometimes I stomp on her feelings, without even thinking,
and she always takes me back, even when I don't deserve it.

Growing up, it was a rare thing to hear an apology; the
dynamic between generations was different then. But today,
it's apparent how far an apology can go toward smoothing
out feelings and leveling the field. If I want my girl to become a woman who's able to admit she's wrong, then I've got
to be…a woman who admits she's wrong as well.

One of the most lovely and strange occurrences I've
noticed over the years is that I'm learning and growing up
alongside my girl. I always thought I would be the one teaching her, but the reverse is more often true than not. This
means that sometimes I make assumptions as well as bad
jokes, or am inconsistent and crabby, and need to ask forgiveness with some regularity. And she rises to the occasion,
forgiving—just as I do with her. It's my hope this give and
take, grounded in love and fluid with grace, will teach us

both how to live and understand better in a world filled with blame and excuses.

In the end, that two-dollar difference in a Safeway deli was really a frugal reminder of an invaluable lesson for us both.

How difficult is it for you to ask forgiveness of your children?

In which instances is it hard to forgive yourself…and what might happen if you did?

ONE VERSE FOR THOUGHT:

Bear with each other and forgive one another if any of you has a grievance against someone. Forgive as the Lord forgave you. **–Colossians 3:13, NIV**

listen up

There was a time when Em was little that I could *uh-huh* my way through her long dissertations about the movie she had just watched or what she'd do if it would finally snow already. Now that she's older, when I hear "Mom? Can I talk to you about something?" I know it's critical that I stop and pay full attention.

We've all experienced being fully heard by someone. Some of us are lucky enough to call that a regular occurrence—no interruption, no hurry, just an inviting, understanding silence that beckons us to stay a while and talk. When you feel lighter at the end of the conversation, you've truly been heard. And for single moms, it seems to be a gift we often give but rarely get to receive: While there's great joy and good in listening to others, we, too, need others who will listen graciously to us.

Sadly, when I need to be heard, I often try to squash the feeling first: I say I am too busy to slow down, too proud to make that call, too strong to open those floodgates. But the past dozen years or so have worn away my edges; I have my God and my friends on the line with some regularity. From divorcing to dieting and loneliness to loss, no topic is off-limits if only I reach out and risk opening myself up.

No doubt these friendships have made me a better mom. From everything my girl has witnessed, she knows the tremendous value of these vulnerable relationships as she and I continue the delicate dance of offering the same to each other in the midst of life's constant transitions. The truth is, some of our closest moments entail one of us not speaking at all.

Let go of the reasons why it's not a convenient time to place that call and bare your soul: It's the sustenance of community that will help you make it in the long run, and I'm almost positive someone's just waiting to hear from you.

Who helps carry the weight of your worries and celebrate your wins?

How does life improve after someone's truly listened to you?

ONE VERSE FOR THOUGHT:
Understand this, my dear brothers and sisters: You must all be quick to listen, slow to speak, and slow to get angry.
–James 1:19, NLT

day five

A couple years ago, we experienced a miracle, right after a catastrophe. My daughter made an inadvertent mistake with a classmate that came across as thoughtless and offensive, things she tries never to be. It was a brutally hard life lesson that involved a lot of tears and waiting: Her heartfelt apology was met with stony silence.

We passed the hours as humans do under such circumstances. We beat ourselves up (Em for the mistake and me for the desire to fix everything). We made ourselves get out of the house. We prayed a lot. We stopped at The Dessert Tray, because sometimes only a giant, chewy peanut butter cookie can help.

And oh Lord, we waited.

In the afternoon of day five, she entered the house doing the I'm-Forgiven-Shimmy. And after I hugged her, I put my hands on her little face and said, "I want you to remember what *this* feels like—this relief that's washing over you. Because someday there will be someone who pisses you off *so bad* you swear you'll never be able to forgive. But *this*? This feeling right here? That's what you'd be giving that person."

I thought of my dear friend who walked me through the hard years after my divorce, who reminded me regularly that I deserved to be a person who not only forgave, but accepted forgiveness as well. It took me years to get that at a cellular level, and I still can hold a grudge with the best of them. I also carry the deep grief of the times my clumsy actions have cost me a friendship, even after the apologies.

But something miraculous happened there on day five that was akin to opening up all the windows and letting a strong breeze blow through: Not only did we get a do-over, it took watching the suffering of the one I love most to see clearly how stingy I myself can be in making way for that cleansing. It was the realest of reminders of what is lost, found, and on the line when it comes to forgiving.

Who needs the gift of forgiveness from you?

And from whom do you need to accept it?

ONE VERSE FOR THOUGHT:
Be kind and compassionate to one another, forgiving each other, just as in Christ God forgave you.
–Ephesians 4:32, NIV

let go of the rope

One of the best and hardest lessons that arose from our Eve's Daughters' co-parenting seminar was that you can't make anyone do anything, let alone what you want them to do. Believe me when I say the air filled with some keening over this bit of reality. Similarly, one of the best and hardest lessons from the Parenting Teens class I took was that I can't make my teen do anything, let alone what I want her to do.

I'm sensing a pattern here.

What gets us in trouble, it seems, is when we're hell-bent on being right and having our way. I have spent years grinding my teeth over the unfairness of the world in general, and of certain individuals in particular. I have thought if I just *explained* things differently the other party might understand and comply. I've even thought perhaps withholding information or affection via the silent treatment might move said person toward my desired outcome. And even when these highly mature and impressive schemes didn't work, I still kept trying, tugging on that knot, determined to bring friends, colleagues, and wayward children over to my side.

I had a situation occur recently that was painfully obvious: I could keep wrenching away, or I could let go of the rope. You'd think it would be easier after marinating in a soup of stubborn people most of my life, but I realized releasing my grip also meant letting go of the satisfaction that comes from justifying. Or vilifying. Or getting the ending I wanted.

I talked with friends; I talked with God. I wished it were different but, in the end, grudgingly, I let go. There's an old saying that suggests you can be right or you can be happy, but you can't be both. Today, I'm no longer right but I'm on my way to happy, and that's progress in my opinion.

Are you cramping up under the weight of your opinions and beliefs? They say expectations are premeditated resentments, and we all could do with fewer of those. Let's practice letting go.

Is there a person or situation you need to release?

How can you teach your children when and how to give in gracefully?

ONE VERSE FOR THOUGHT:
A fool takes no pleasure in understanding, but only in expressing his opinion. **–Proverbs 18:2, ESV**

death and life

I was driving recently, cooling my heels at a red light, when I looked in the rearview mirror and saw what looked like my father in the car behind me. My heart pounded as I gaped, because he died in a car accident in 2009. It was just another one of those weird sightings I've had in the years since his death; I should be used to them, but they always catch me off-guard. I've been fatherless seven years, technically speaking, but based on our rocky relationship, it's been far longer than that. The strange thing is I am still acutely aware of having one less layer of protection in the world, even though I stopped needing a dad long ago.

After my dad died, I spoke with a pastor about missing that feeling of security. He commented dryly that single parenthood isn't a very sexy cause, so to speak, but that single parents impact us all—individually, societally, corporately. We need to be committed to them, to each other and to a sense of security, even though our lives aren't terribly glamorous, even though it's often a slog, day in, day out, first right, then left. I know a little more about my father now that he's passed. I know more about the reasons why, perhaps, he didn't have it in him to do the daily slog with me. And I know God in His mercy has seen fit to give me the best rental dads a girl could ask for.

Still, it hasn't lessened the ache I feel some days.

Friends who've lost parents have been especially tender with me, knowing the questioning, understanding the floundering, and for that I'm especially grateful. But as much as I've wished for a different ending with him, I know I must continue contributing to a different ending of my own.

Maybe we single parents will get to the point where there's more community and less polarity, where we'll better relate to others' miles-traveled marathons instead of doing a perfunctory check-in. Maybe our glamour-less status will become ironic in that we'll find we have each other, and that's a thing of true beauty. Perhaps most important, those relationships themselves will create another layer of protection: of caring, of concern, of listening, laughing, crying, walking and *living* in an uncertain world.

Who provides those layers of protection for you as a single parent?

How have you grieved the big losses in your life?

ONE VERSE FOR THOUGHT:
He heals the brokenhearted and binds up their wounds.
–Psalm 147:3, NASB

shifting gears

In a radical act (radical for me, anyway) I have taken some time off. I'm not going anywhere and I'm not doing anything special, but I recognized I needed to move from my normal rolling boil to a slow simmer. It's hard for me to slow down, but recent years and various health challenges have required it and when I ignore it…well, there's the same fallout that happens whenever one ignores problems. I have long tried to serve from a practically empty vessel, and not only does it frustrate and weaken me, it shortchanges the people I want to pour into—from my daughter and family to friends, co-workers, and Eve's Daughters' moms.

A million years ago, during the initially terrifying experience of learning to drive a stick shift auto, my father reminded me about the importance of listening to the engine; when it started straining under too much effort, it was time to shift gears. After accidentally terrorizing a few pedestrians in cross walks and brutalizing the engine a bit, I started to get it: First gear is great when you're just getting started, but it's not going to work for you when you're cruising down the interstate at 70 miles per hour.

As in driving, what gets us started in life often isn't the same thing that takes us where we ultimately need to go. Single moms tend to run on all cylinders, all of the time, but when we start to feel the strain—the annoyance, exhaustion and ambivalence—a big change is in order. When you're used to revving at high RPMs most of the time, sometimes it's wisest to *downshift*.

In a most unrelaxing twist during my down-time, I'm also teaching my daughter to drive. I told a friend that she's as tight as a piano wire in these early hours on the road. I'm grateful for her caution but also recognize she will have to loosen up as she gains those miles; otherwise, she'll feel overwhelmed and unable to continue.

In her case, lightening up will take her far. As, hopefully, it will you and me.

What and who help fill your tank?

How does your family respond when you're able to downshift and enjoy a slower pace?

ONE VERSE FOR THOUGHT:
I'll refresh tired bodies; I'll restore tired souls.
–Jeremiah 31:25, MSG

wishing well

I have sat with and listened to literally hundreds of single moms and, in my own experience and theirs, I've come to believe two of the most life-stopping words are "I wish":

I wish we could have worked it out.

I wish he'd just pay his child support.

I wish we could be more civil to each other.

I wish she could be supportive instead of judgmental.

We can spend so much time wishing that we never settle into a deep appreciation of what is...only a deep dissatisfaction of what isn't. If your children's father didn't respect you during your time as a couple, he likely won't respect you any more during and after your uncoupling. If your mother's never been supportive, if your sister's always been so dang competitive, if your children aren't appreciative, wishing it were different will not make it so.

I spent many seasons of my life in a state of perpetual victimhood, planning for how awesome life would be as soon as everyone around me behaved. Many years, tears, and miles later, I now guarantee life doesn't work this way; *wishin' and hopin'* are simply great euphemisms for *not moving*. And, ladies—don't we wish to *move*?

Gratefully, time is on our side in this instance. After listening to a litany of my *I-wishes*, a dear friend once pointed out that certain challenges, like so much gum on our shoes, pop up repeatedly so we get another chance to deal with them in a healthier manner. She compared it to traveling a spiral staircase; each step of growth and maturity changes our vantage point so, while we circle back to the same problems, we have a different view.

What I know for sure is that I have zero control over others, so wishing for different behavior from them is futile. All I can do is adjust (or, better yet, get rid of) my expectations for anything different and focus on what is in my control: how I choose to behave, how I choose to react, and how I choose to move forward without said wishes coming true.

For us to truly wish *well*, we need to understand what's in our power to change and what isn't...and let the latter go.

What is one of your biggest wishes that will never come true?

In what ways can you get what you need without relying on others changing their behavior?

ONE VERSE FOR THOUGHT:
And don't be wishing you were someplace else or with someone else. Where you are right now is God's place for you. Live and obey and love and believe right there...
–1 Corinthians 7:17, MSG

wistmastime is here

I always get a little wistful/weepy/whelmed during the win-
ter holidays. Part of it is how I'm wired, and part of it is that
it's just too dang much: too much to do, see, eat, buy, wrap,
spend, plan. *What should be* repeatedly bumps up against *what
is*. While I've made my peace with the fact that my life is not
a Hallmark commercial, I do often long for the calm that's
depicted (or manufactured, as the case may be) on TV—
happy kids, toasty fire, darling retriever that doesn't snore or
fart even *once*, like mine does.

Single moms can feel stretched even thinner than usual
during this time of year, not to mention stressed over commitments, finances, sharing time with a former partner, and
their kids' well-being. For many years, I fell into a bad pattern
of trying to really whip things into a froth for my daughter to
mitigate the fact her parents were divorced. While I couldn't
pull it off financially speaking (because we simply didn't have
it), I did try really hard to "make some Christmas magic"
on numerous occasions and, frankly, burned myself out. My
wild activity added little to my daughter's well-being, and
her lack of appreciation for my holiday gymnastics left me a
tinge—how shall we say?—resentful.

After several Christmases that kind of crashed and burned,
I learned to scale back—to neatly lay out my plans (usually
terribly unrealistic)…and then cut them by about two-thirds.
I push myself to call friends, especially other single moms,
when I'm feeling lonely and loser-like for not pulling off the
Traditional American Holidays (As Seen On TV). I talk to
myself as I did to my daughter when she was young: *Are
you hungry? Thirsty? Tired? Wired?* And then—what a con-

cept!—I take care of those basic needs. It's astounding how much more doable life becomes with a little protein and a 20-minute nap.

There's much we can do to make certain seasons easier… because the trick to keeping life manageable is *inside us*.

How have you learned to de-stress the holidays?

What do your kids really expect out of the holidays, and what do you assume they expect?

ONE VERSE FOR THOUGHT:
Better a dry crust with peace and quiet than a house full of feasting, with strife. **–Proverbs 17:1, NIV**

heart of stone

At my fourth birthday gathering, I received a heart-shaped gold locket which, by party's end, was lost. My parents angrily demanded I retrace my steps but, despite my time and tears, it was gone. Then, when I was fourteen, my father called me outside as he resurfaced the driveway and dropped into my hand that old locket—scratched, bent and nicked, having been run over thousands of times by cars, snow blowers, bicycles, roller skates and more. That heart had seen better days for sure, but the locket still opened under tender pressure.

Now, in my fifties, I'm sensing my heavenly father is telling me to retrace my steps and find the most valuable heart I lost—the soft one—because it seems He and I cannot go forward without it. This heart, too, has been hammered by outside forces, run over and dinged pretty good. Throughout a long, painful divorce and many challenging years as a single mom, I admit I have not been as interested in redemption as I have been in protection. *Change* and *growth* are so much harder than *ease* and *safety*...and I'm sure I'm not the only one who feels this way.

God's promise to redeem us, to remove our hearts of stone and replace them with hearts of flesh, is one of those double-edged deals. On one hand, for those of us who've felt raked over the coals by life and circumstance, harder hearts fool us into thinking we're protected, prevent us from truly feeling, and convince us we're in control. On the other, hearts of flesh are soft and squishy and malleable, able to be stretched and contorted every which way; these hearts don't even pretend to know all the answers. If we agree to this redemption process, our armored center will be stripped away and the possibility of being wounded from the pain of life seems very real. But the question remains: What kind of life do we want? And which heart should lead the way?

As I've searched for my true heart, I've also had the privilege of sitting with others as they study theirs. I've had women before me, weeping, wondering: Their hearts have been broken—badly—and they're not sure they'll ever feel whole again. Another friend muses aloud, trying to determine exactly when and how he got so lost. The tears come, the heads shake: There are no good answers. But when we can truly *be* with each other and sit quietly and listen, we begin to appreciate the very thing we've feared all our lives: being so transparent. It's only when our armor drops that our hearts of flesh can shine through.

What could being more tenderhearted do for you and your children?

How can you help your kids search for their true hearts?

ONE VERSE FOR THOUGHT:

And I will give them one heart, and put a new spirit within them. And I will take the heart of stone out of their flesh and give them a heart of flesh… **–Ezekiel 11:19, NASB**

3

one dose of reality

ON LETTING GO,
TAKING CHANCES, AND
LIVING LIFE ON LIFE'S TERMS

strong enough to cry

It's been hitting me hard in recent weeks: we're moving into the soon-to-be-lasts. The soon-to-be last school year. The soon-to-be last caramel apple run at the local farms. The soon-to-be last Christmas Peanuts/Grinch/Rudolph marathon. Gah—then prom! And graduation!! Where in the world did the time go? The days are a thousand hours long but the years fly by.

At dinner recently, I tried to tell Em how it was just seemingly a few months ago that I was reading **Barbie as the Princess and the Pauper** to her while she was in the tub, to ensure she wouldn't drown, and now we're up to our elbows in SATs and college applications. Instead, I started to cry. I told her how I feared I wouldn't be enough, and that she wouldn't turn out right, and that it would all be my fault because I got a divorce. Instead, she's turning into a remarkable young woman. Then she started to cry. Then we both started to laugh. Then the dog looked at us as if we were nuts, but with such a crazy, improbable turn of events, the tears are gonna flow. Still, I wanted to stop short of apologizing for it.

For so many years, I was always so sorry for my tears—sorry for embarrassing myself, sorry for making others uncomfortable. But the older I get, the more I believe that tears are a sign of strength, not weakness. It means I've been through some stuff and made it out the other side, paradoxically stronger and softer simultaneously, without shutting down my heart. I always smile a bit, kindly, when I ask single moms how they're doing and they leak out all the pressures they're under—the uncertainties, the lack of money, the kids who are acting up—and then apologize for their crying. Well, why wouldn't they cry? They're carrying a huge load, and they (like I) want the best for their kids. Sometimes it seems so overwhelming and hopeless they've got to let the tears out and then, afterwards, it somehow seems doable again.

I don't know about you, but I have told myself, "This is impossible—we will never make it" about a million times during my single mom journey. But day after day, step after step, somehow we keep going. So, yeah—single parents are sort of doing the impossible…and a few tears are allowed.

I hope that every hard-earned tear is viewed as precious, because it is. It means you're not shutting down, tuning out, or giving up, but instead living life with an open heart (and showing your kids how to do that, too). If that's not worthy of a 21-Kleenex® salute, I don't know what is.

What do you think would happen if you didn't censor your tears?

How can you encourage your children to honor their emotions—even the hard ones?

ONE VERSE FOR THOUGHT:
Those who plant in tears will harvest with shouts of joy.
–Psalm 126:5, NLT

vaguely familiar

Over the years, with some regularity, I have gotten to the point where I could no longer stand the state of my daughter's room. When she was younger, I'd suggest we clean. Well, *I'd* start cleaning and guilt her into joining me. Once she entered her room and motioned to the open window.

"Mom, it's freezing in here."

"Yes, my little petri dish, but this open window is keeping me alive," I said as I swept my fingers over her bookshelf and created a Pigpen-style cloud of dust. "Where'd we put the haz mat gear?"

After she finished rolling her eyes, she'd start cleaning as well and it would dawn on me: I must have gotten the wrong baby at the hospital. Because I actually like it neat and tidy, you know, relatively speaking. And that thought led to the next, of the many ways she and I are different, how weird that is, and how much, frankly, *I've* had to change in raising her. Just saying. She's not having to change, I am. And I wonder if she'll ever know *me*...or just me as Mom.

Nothing wears away our rough edges like parenting, because where else can we feel so inept, out-of-control, and at a loss on our way toward becoming better human beings? Throughout the years, I've become a more patient me, a more selfless me, but that change always comes with a steep cost. As a single mom, I liken this to feeling my way around a dark room, trying to get my bearings without another important adult there to shed some light or provide a clear reflection. You can end up bumping into things—emotions, feelings, dust and dirty socks—and it's up to you to figure out how you're going to handle it.

We have entered a strange new time, she and I, where we butt heads as often as we hold hands. She's pulling away, wondering who she'll become as she grows up.

I, too, wonder what I will become as less Mom, more Me.

In what ways are your children similar to you?

Which traits of theirs drive you crazy…and do you have the same behaviors yourself?

ONE VERSE FOR THOUGHT:
Parents, don't come down too hard on your children or you'll crush their spirits. **–Colossians 3:21, MSG**

risky business

Recently, a friend of mine relayed a comment made by a famous woman who's in the process of reinventing herself at midlife. The gist was that women need to let their daughters see them taking risks...and even see them fail (and of course, this goes for sons as well). The "gift" of failing, after you finish nursing your bruises, frees our most-loveds to fail themselves and learn that it's rarely fatal.

For anyone who knows me, it should go without saying that I'm not referring to heli-skiing, mountaineering, or deep-water scuba-type risks. I'm talking about starting that business, moving to another state (or country), living alone even though you're scared or lonely, giving so much that you're always living on the edge, or (gasp) embracing fifty and beyond.

I've always tended toward the orderly and predictable, preferring life to be on the neater side. But I'm also a very strong woman on a lot of levels. So why, then, do I want to show my daughter only the clean side, the pain-free side? Often, it's because I want her to feel safe, and that is a good thing...to a point. Because we live in an unsafe place where bad things happen to innocent people and longings go unanswered and people up and die, there's only so much safety I can provide. Do I want her to think well of me (by keeping everything neat and in control) or would I rather she think well of herself ("If Mom can do a face plant in life and keep going, so can I")?

The older I get, the freer I get, and the freer I get, the more I can share the real me with my girl. I'm less afraid of telling her the times I've been terrified; I'm no longer searching for the perfect answer, instead telling her I've often been unclear. This frees her to go through life wondering, questioning. Risking. Life is indeed risky business—how are you living it?

When have you been able to be "answerless" to your kids—to honestly say you don't know something?

How can your transparency enable your children to take more age-appropriate risks in life?

ONE VERSE FOR THOUGHT:
I can do all things through him who strengthens me.
–Philippians 4:13, ESV

the sisterhood of the
traveling brain

So many of my sisters—accomplished women of my age—have complained lately of their propensity towards brainlessness. Is it our age? Circumstances? Hormonal imbalances? All I can say is it seems we only have one brain between us, and we're passing it around when we could or should be using it. Mind you, I am privileged to hang with a really talented group of women, so we are all terribly chagrined about this sudden scourge of intelligence.

I regularly sit in my office, eyes rolling toward the ceiling, trying to capture a word...begins with a *p...p p ppppa*. This wouldn't be so bad if I didn't make my living as a writer. And when the other thoughts fly in—*need dental floss, E's evening performance, sugar-free chocolate*—I take dictation on my little lime green Post-It® pad. It's come down to this: a life in stickies.

My daughter finds this hysterical—the notes stuck to the coffee pot, the calendar, the mirror. I glare at her and say I didn't used to be this way, before I was a mom, and warn that her time is coming. Also that it's her fault. I used to have a life, a fully firing brain and goals. Not anymore. And it's been a bittersweet adjustment.

What I am realizing, however, is that it's all a trade-off. I had my daughter at thirty-four, and what I lost in energy from my twenties, I (hopefully) gained in patience and common sense in my thirties. Paradoxically, I'm realizing my calling to raise my daughter proficiently necessitated I lose some of my previous efficiency. Sometimes less is more, if you know what I mean. This journey is requiring a transparency, a realness, a humility I didn't use to have—which I would have been embarrassed to have, actually—in my youth. To make it through single motherhood, I had to lose some of my polish to earn a different kind of glow—the kind that comes from recognizing we're indeed growing older, but perhaps deeper and more beautiful, less afraid and rigid. This impacts our work, our relationships, and our mothering, but I find I have less to prove these days, and that, in itself, is pretty freeing.

What have been some of the personality trade-offs you've experienced as you raise your children alone over time?

Which youthful flaws have you been happy to send on their way?

ONE VERSE FOR THOUGHT:

That is why we are not discouraged. Though outwardly we are wearing out, inwardly we are renewed day by day.
–2 Corinthians 4:16, GW

easy does it

I got to spend time with an old, old friend recently—one who knows so much about me that we simply pick up where we left off. In the years since we've seen each other, we've navigated our kids' middle- and high-school transitions, full-time employment, relational quandaries, second-floor bathroom overflows that require holes cut into first-floor ceilings, and dying and aging parents, among other topics. There's an absence of judgment and an abundance of laughter. My petite blonde friend is raising three active boys, so her looks deceive: She has a core of titanium underneath the slim exterior.

We laughed about how lax we've become as the years pass. What once would have sent us in a panic to the ER now merits an unsterile Band-Aid®, haphazardly applied. The further I slog down the Mommy Superhighway, I'm finding I know less, not more. I thought my utter dedication and tireless supervision would keep life in line, but there's so much over which we have zero control. Seasons pass, my girl's heart gets bruised with some regularity, plans change, people leave, life is terribly unfair. Any ideas about control have been outgrown as quickly as my daughter's t-shirts and leggings.

I wish someone would have told me earlier that diligence is fine and all, but Easy Does It should be the single mom's mantra. I think I'd have fewer gray hairs, less stress, and more good memories. I wouldn't have gone as ballistic years ago when I saw my then-toddler sharing her ice cream with the dog (one lick for her, one lick for him), or as wigged out over a 104-degree temp that barely slowed her down.

I'm hopeful, as parenthood progresses, that my daughter and I will have more stories based in an easier-going reality—of times when cereal suffices for dinner, when cleaning the toilet gets waylaid for a game of tickle, when an outing for $1 ice cream is doable even on the tightest budget. When Easy Does It becomes a way of life.

How have you needed to simplify as a single parent?

How could "Easy Does It" be applied to your life now?

ONE VERSE FOR THOUGHT:
For everything there is a season, and a time for every matter under heaven. **–Ecclesiastes 3:1, ESV**

the amazing invisible woman

One of my single mom friends has kids involved in sports and, as it often happens, she finds herself transporting other kids to and from practices as well, which she does happily and willingly. But she relayed that, while picking her son up from a play date recently, some of the other sports parents she knew—whose children she had tended to, provided snacks for and transported to events—started arriving at the very same home with items for a potluck…to which she and her son clearly had not been invited. My heart broke for her, as I've been in that exact situation: You're desperately trying to keep those stinging tears from showing and protect your kid's heart while getting the unwanted but absolute confirmation that your little family is somehow less-than.

Of the many challenges we discuss as single parents, this is perhaps one of the hardest: There are no tools, tips or techniques to garnering invitations or being included. For me, this has been one of the more painful things to accept. I joke that, for a woman of my size, there's no way I could be invisible. But, mostly, I am; after all these years, we have but a precious few families who continue to invite and include us. Somehow, single parents are largely invisible to the greater population. To me, this is heartbreaking because it occurs at the time when we most desperately need to be seen, when loss and change have rocked our foundations.

It is so easy as a single parent to just put your head down and work away, feeling alone, alienated, forgotten, dismissed. Invisible. But within a community of single parents, with something as simple as sharing a meal along with our hearts, we get to see and be seen for the most beautiful reasons.

There are times it still hurts my heart (even after 15 years of single momdom) that I am not included or invited to events given by people who would say they are my friends. I've come to believe that you can't really understand unless you are suddenly single yourself. But that shouldn't preclude us from creating and celebrating in a community of our own making. We need each other, and we need to *see* each other.

What can you do to foster a single parent community?

How can you help your kids plug in and feel included?

ONE VERSE FOR THOUGHT:
Don't forget to show hospitality to strangers, for some who have done this have entertained angels without realizing it! **–Hebrews 13:2, NLT**

mystery mom

I still laugh when I think of her reaction—my daughter's wide eyes when she heard I'd won some awards for my writing, and her subsequent disbelief when I told her they were in a box somewhere in the garage. I may as well have told her I spent my twenties as a Nobel-winning supermodel; her shock was both amusing and telling.

How can you live with someone for years and have them know absolutely *nothing* about you?

There was a time when my life was much harder, when the fallout of the divorce made me want to protect Em from my thoughts and emotions. In an attempt to shield her from grief and pain, I also hid much of what makes me me, so all she saw was the maker of rolly pancakes and the One Who Demands a Clean Room. No wonder anything outside those roles was startling—I was not being entirely honest with her.

Someone much wiser than I described the gift we give our kids when we're really *real* with them. Of course discretion is key, but somehow it evens the playing field for them to know that we also hated math, got our hearts broken, struggled with self-esteem, and cried ourselves to sleep…maybe even (or especially) if that's happened recently.

As Emma gets older, I've taken many a deep breath and shared from my heart…things I hope for, things I regret, things that happened to make me who I am. Some of these things are not neat and pretty, but she is learning to be transparent and vulnerable and hopeful by witnessing my own attempts at the same.

Maybe you used to sing or do karate. Maybe you had a crush on someone who made fun of you, or you couldn't climb the rope in gym class either. Maybe you have dreams of going back to school or to Paris. What can you share with your kids that will make you really real...that will make their eyes bug and their mouths drop?

Let your kids know some of your past and your dreams, and watch those conversations bring you even closer.

Are you able to share with your kids who you are, versus what you do?

Which parts of you would most surprise your kids?

ONE VERSE FOR THOUGHT:

You are the light of the world. A city set on a hill cannot be hidden. Nor do people light a lamp and put it under a basket, but on a stand, and it gives light to all in the house.
–Matthew 5:14-15, ESV

weakness wins

Many modern-day experts counsel today's leaders to tap into the power that comes from weakness. But in parenting, as in business, this seems counterintuitive. How many of us bend the truth, manipulate circumstances to protect our kids from hurt, or prevent them from seeing us struggle?

In solo parenting, strength wins, right?

Well, we recently had one death and three cancer diagnoses within days of each other, and let me just say: strength didn't win. Instead, Em and I cried and railed and wondered. We talked about circling the wagons with these friends, giving them a soft spot to land, and bringing casseroles, black humor, prayers, and all the hope we could muster over the long haul. We spoke about the crazy-making not-knowing of why a good God allows lousy things to happen. But mostly, we talked about how unpredictable and messy life and love can be…and how we need to walk through it anyway.

As our kids get older, it's of paramount importance to them to appear as perfect and together as possible. Nothing is more embarrassing than not knowing something or fumbling when you should be smooth. While I get this (and still wrestle with it myself at times), my heart aches for my daughter because it's a hard lesson to learn—that of letting go and bumbling about as you find your way. As adults, we often are forced to give up this quest for perfection, and it can be an awkward, painful process…so it's hard to watch our kids follow in those footprints. But loving (and living) with a limp means you're finally becoming real: We need help from others, and they from us. In this regard, weakness wins.

If I had a do-over, I think I'd say "I don't know" a lot earlier and a lot more often. I think I'd protect my girl less from the hurt and pray more that it would shape her into the woman she's supposed to become. And for myself, I think I'd try to fear the mess less and demonstrate how to love well in the midst of it.

In which areas of your life are you afraid to be less than proficient?

What might happen if you demonstrated weakness to your children?

ONE VERSE FOR THOUGHT:

But he told me: "My kindness is all you need. My power is strongest when you are weak." So I will brag even more about my weaknesses in order that Christ's power will live in me. **–2 Corinthians 12:9, GW**

a different kind of good

Since our most promising college visit in September, I've watched my girl get more and more excited, focused, and hopeful. The early admissions application was sent with great fanfare recently, and now we wait to hear.

At one of her recent color guard competitions, signs hung in the school's hallways that read "Did you do anything to prepare for college today?" And I thought, "No…but I'd like to!" Truth is, I wish I were going to college. OK, not really—college was a miserable time for me, frankly—but I wish for the adventure of something new, of something that would stretch me and grow me and start churning up this seemingly stagnant water I've been treading for some time now.

As I watch her readying to spread her wings, I want what I have to not be all there is.

I am beyond excited for her, but I also recognize that I am old and crusty and war-worn and I know too much for my own good. I know the best-laid plans can go haywire. I know that "endless love" can break your heart. I know that good dreams can die bad deaths way too young, and that God's calling is amazing but so much harder and less glamorous than we'd expect. I know the end of high school is only the beginning of her second act, but she does not.

But, Moms? We kinda know what's coming. The break-ups. The questions. The bad decisions. The fallout from the bad decisions. We of all people know what can happen, and yet: Somehow, some way, we have to let them hope big and hard on everything that awaits…even though we know how fickle life can be. The alternative is to be bitter and miserable and girding our loins at every turn for the worst to happen, and that is its own special hell.

Instead, I'm trying hard to appreciate the shine of hope in her eyes while thinking about the tears at graduation, for the classmates she might not see again. I think about her leaving. I think about her being sick the first time away from home. I think about classroom struggles and bad grades and her moving to Japan. And I think there's not much I can do about any of it, other than change my mindset to believe a different kind of good is coming—for us both. It is most assuredly true that life is hard, but I also have to believe that God is good...from our first act all the way through to our finale.

How do you temper your knowledge of life's difficulties against your kids' hopes?

What dreams do you have for yourself, in your next act?

ONE VERSE FOR THOUGHT:
I pray that God, the source of hope, will fill you completely with joy and peace because you trust in him. Then you will overflow with confident hope through the power of the Holy Spirit. **–Romans 15:13, NLT**

waiting in the dark

When I was going through my divorce, I knew one single mom—my friend and business partner, Cathy. It sounds weird, but she truly saw me at a time when I felt invisible. When I was terrified of the future, she'd talk me down. When I was spending the equivalent of a second mortgage in child-care each month, Cathy gave me her daughter's hand-me-downs. She is generous and awesome and trust me when I say you wish she was your friend, too. But I digress.

When I "got the call" (spiritually speaking) to help birth Eve's Daughters, it came after a year of me being a cheer-leader for Cathy because, actually, it was *her* idea. Well, funny how God works. When I knew it was time for us to join forces, I cried for an entire weekend (true story). She felt the same nudge and spent the same weekend playing Solitaire and ignoring my multiple phone calls. I guess we all deal with reality in different ways. We laugh now, but the idea of creating Eve's Daughters—a true community for single moms and their children—was overwhelming. We had no idea what God had planted.

What I've learned is, God seems to do His best work in the dark. Despite being common, we single moms are invis-ible…and when you're invisible, it can sure feel like you're out there swinging on your own. But in community, we have each other, and God himself is with us, in us, and it's never more apparent than in Advent—the season of waiting. We wait for our circumstances to change, for more money to ar-rive, for our kids to be OK. We wait for biopsy results and we wait for peace. But do not forget in all this waiting there's something readying to be born.

Many of us struggle through the holidays. But I wish for us to wait well in the darkness for the light that's going to come. Silently, invisibly, you are doing what it takes to nurture your babies so they carry all kinds of good into the world.

What are you waiting for?

In which instances has something good been born out of a period of your suffering?

ONE VERSE FOR THOUGHT:
I know the plans that I have for you, declares the Lord. They are plans for peace and not disaster, plans to give you a future filled with hope. **–Jeremiah 29:11, GW**

4

one good cry

ON GRIEVING WELL, MAKING PEACE, AND MOVING ON

the cleansing

The Pacific Northwest is not the place to make your home if you have an aversion to water. We are smack in the middle of January—the month with 171 days—and it is wet and gray with rain pelting sideways, and now a mysterious roof leak is adding to my jumbled, damp mood, further proving that grief and suffering hit at the most inopportune times.

Once, in the immediate aftermath of my divorce, I remember reading one of humorist Dave Barry's articles and practically wetting myself, just howling with laughter…until I totally collapsed in sobs. The transformation took about two seconds and was, frankly, kind of unnerving. In the years since, I've seemingly taken up crying as a hobby, much as someone might glom onto scrapbooking. There have been times when I've asked Him to just take me Home, because life here can be so excruciatingly disappointing, especially when *life* happens over and over. Once when I did this, I was laying on my bed, crying, exhausted, and I must have fallen asleep. A short time later I awoke with a groan, thinking, "Aw, *hell*. I'm still *here*. May as well throw in a load."

For years I held the opinion that crying was for the weak. I was raised to believe that I had no good reason to cry and, if I continued, I would indeed be given a good reason. So I just clamped down and clammed up and didn't allow myself to feel anything. But forty or so years' worth of pent-up grief puts you behind the eight ball; that's when a little roof leak can make you take to your bed with a warehouse-store carton of tissues.

When we come ungracefully to the ends of ourselves— when we can't control roof leaks or divorces or wayward kids—is that when we finally meet God? Because it seems all the finagling and control must give way first…and the second-to-last stop prior to meeting Him can involve a lot of tears.

It is rare these days that I can get through an entire worship service at church without leaking. I can't explain it, but when I can't form the words, the tears seem to do it. Maybe it takes being completely emptied before we get it—that our brokenness is our engraved invitation to come before Him, that our tears become the Housewarming gift we bring. Maybe it's the simple act of showing up, soggy though we may be, that tempers the ache. My job is to not have the answers, and it's not to stop the tears. He just asks me to be present. And I know He'll be present again. That is enough.

When you don't let yourself grieve, what happens?

How do you make your tears OK with your kids?

ONE VERSE FOR THOUGHT:
You keep track of all my sorrows. You have collected all my tears in your bottle. You have recorded each one in your book. **–Psalm 56:8, NLT**

good byes

If you're reading this, you're alive; and if you're alive, you've likely gone through a forced separation of some sort—a death, a friendship ending, a divorce or breakup, the kind that leaves you doubled-over and reeling. My friend Deby shared a graphic from The Writer's Circle that blows the old five stages of grief out of the water, as it includes many disconcerting occurrences such as emotional outbursts, disorganization, isolation, and more. Depicted in the shape of an inverse omega, the graphic shows how grief takes us way down into the pit before we can climb out the other side. Of all we can feel, grief surely must be the iceberg of emotions, with so very much roiling under the surface.

But one characteristic Deby highlighted is panic, saying it's one of the hardest to articulate. As soon as I read her comment, it was my gut—an immediate clench—that took me back to those wrenching days and nights during my long divorce. There were the night terrors over losing my kid, my house, my ability to work. There were dark daydreams of drowning in bitterness so deep I'd stay in the muck forever. And, of course, no matter how crazy the thought: *whatever will I do without this person?* Whether it's love or hate, from friends to parents to spouses, we cannot imagine going on…so when the ax falls, from disillusionment, disgust or death, we gasp for breath and wonder whether the sun will ever rise again.

In keeping company now with several friends deep in the pit, I am reminded that grief is not something we're taught to do well in America and, oh, how we shortchange ourselves because of it. Our ability to grieve and mourn is directly proportional to our ability to love and connect; we cannot have one without the other. We can keep too busy to break down, stick our heads in the sand to ignore the impending disaster, or go kicking and screaming into that dark night, but it *will* catch up with us down the road…through bitterness of spirit, dwindling health, or the never-ending ache of loss unexamined.

Of the many things I'd do over, perhaps the most strange would be to demonstrate my new-found willingness to dive headfirst into that dark pool so I could break the surface so much faster than I did in the past. Even now, as I navigate relationships and lives that are shifting and ending, I want my *byes* to be truly *good*.

Go deep. Deeper still. Your grief will not last forever, but the gifts from it will.

Do you welcome, wallow in, or run from grief?

What kind of growth and wisdom have come from your darkest seasons of loss?

ONE VERSE FOR THOUGHT:
Even in the unending shadows of death's darkness, I am not overcome by fear. Because You are with me in those dark moments, near with Your protection and guidance, I am comforted. **–Psalm 23:4, VOICE**

today

The recent death of a high school friend has me looking backward and forward simultaneously. For me, high school was just a couple years ago, or so it seems. Death is especially poignant when it's someone *your* age, and when you realize that enough time has passed so *your children* are in high school. This particular friend was part of a group of seven or eight of us who clung to each other throughout all the ups and downs of high school—from family dramas to questionable boyfriends to bad test results and far more. In the years since, some of us drifted apart and others still are in touch. But with our friend's death, it was hard for me to stay in the day. While digging for my yearbooks to reminisce, I moved a box and found Em's "What I Looked Like in First Grade" folder. Suffice it to say, she doesn't look like that anymore.

Honestly, I'm embarrassed to say I've spent most of my days looking elsewhere. I tend toward romanticizing the past or envisioning the future. It's always seemed like today's not exciting enough, not juicy enough. But, after what feels like a million boring todays, my daughter's in high school, and I'm finding myself less inclined to push forward as that means her driving. Dating. Leaving! I am thrilled for her to discover her life and I won't be hanging onto her ankles, but it will be a big change indeed when she's out of the house. It's been so bittersweet to contemplate my little buddy not being here every day to plan with, banter with, and eat with. What will *that* today look like?

After all these years of racing ahead, my challenge now is to appreciate the ordinary: the loud and the quiet, the messy and the unknown, the sweetness of her still grabbing my hand sometimes as we walk, and the seriousness of discussing boys and finals and God. Maybe it's been long-term exhaustion and questions and fear that have pushed me unrelentingly toward the future, toward a time I always imagined would be easier, but how many unrepeatable moments have I missed in that process?

How strange that it's taken this much time to appreciate it, when today has been here all along.

How can you practice mindfulness—that is, staying in the now—while raising your kids?

In what ways can you share with your children about being present, and being grateful for it?

ONE VERSE FOR THOUGHT:
So do not worry about tomorrow; for tomorrow will care for itself. Each day has enough trouble of its own.
–Matthew 6:34, NASB

fatherless but fathered

When I returned from my dad's memorial service in Chicago, I knew more than on any other trip that "home," in terms of people, was gone and I wouldn't get a do-over. But finally, after years of yearning, I was OK with that ending.

It used to be every time I went back to the Midwest I had a fidgety sense of wanting to fix things, as though I could take one more whack at restoring relationships or getting people to understand. While I loved my earthly dad, in the end I could not have a relationship with him. It cost us both too much. I love him still and hope more than anything that the restless man I knew is at peace.

I have worn my fatherlessness since he died like an ill-fitting garment. Sometimes it chafed, squeezing too tightly, and sometimes it was too airy with all those unsettled differences still hovering between us. It's taken some getting used to but I've tried to keep my eyes on God, tried to keep asking and listening and moving and living.

I smile to think I now have two fathers in heaven, totally, wildly different. One has a much more colorful vocabulary than the other, for example. Occasionally I'll watch the photo slide show from my dad's service, hear the old Neil Diamond song I suggested play in the background, and just cry. I have ached to have a last conversation with my dad, one that worked, but now I just kind of talk to him during the day, as I do with my other Father. I wish I could hear something back from either party, but I think it was Oswald Chambers who wrote something to the effect that we grow to the point where God trusts us with His silences. Generally, I wish not to be so trustworthy in these types of situations, but for now, silence it is.

And in the midst of all this processing, life keeps happening: We've continued growing Eve's Daughters in fits and starts, people come and go, my daughter gets taller and wiser, things are breaking left and right, friends suffer and celebrate and we keep shuffling left/right/left. But something has shifted in this latest process: I *know* without a doubt Em and I are being watched over. Silently, lovingly, eternally. For all the years I ached for my father, I'm finding the old vulnerability is gone. I think that's one of the smallest and biggest things we can hope for in this world—to matter to someone else, but to also know the cost of aloneness and, therefore, develop the empathy to want to help pay someone else's way. And that, in itself, can give life.

How do you keep living in the midst of bouts of grief?

Have you found yourself in recent years more or less likely to take the risk of being close to others?

ONE VERSE FOR THOUGHT:
You, Lord, keep my lamp burning; my God turns my darkness into light. **–Psalm 18:28, NIV**

exploring the depths

I watched Pixar's amazing *Inside Out* recently and was astounded at how the movie's writers so creatively tackled such an abstract concept as our emotions. Perhaps most touching was the notion that sadness is, necessarily, nearby in life, waiting in the wings, if only to make opposing emotions such as joy and relief that much more pronounced.

In therapy after my divorce, I was given an 8.5-by-11-inch page with multiple columns of "feeling" words...things like *overwhelmed* and *dumbfounded*, *outraged* and *wistful*. With the exception of sad and mad (which I'm chagrined to report I had down-pat), I had suppressed so many of my emotions for so long I didn't even know what was going on under the surface. So when my counselor asked, "What are you feeling today?" I felt like a little kid in a guessing game. "Um," I said, tracing my finger down the lines of words, "...*moody*? Maybe...a little *dejected*?" It's taken a lot of years to stop when I'm angry or sad and ask: *What's* really *going on*? It feels a little silly to talk to myself like I'm a toddler, but behind the anger and the sadness I've re-discovered fear, rejection, loneliness, shame...a plethora of emotions that can lead me, paradoxically, to better mental health if I take the time to explore them. Even better, this practice also has helped me become more aware of delight, contentedness and gratitude...no matter how fleeting.

Maybe you grew up in a family that prized joy. Maybe, when confronted with a sad you, those same adults promised to give you something to *really* cry about if you didn't knock it off. Such behavior was common of that generation; for myriad reasons (and probably very few of those healthy ones), melancholy wasn't allowed. But to fully appreciate our emotions, we have to be willing to consider *all* of them worthy of exploration—to let them see the light of day and understand what they're trying to tell us—instead of sending them to the dark cellar of our subconscious, uninvestigated.

Our amazing Eve's Daughters moms have been strong enough and generous enough to share with each other the entire gamut of feelings—from rage and despair to hope and courage. They've created a safe space in which to do so, and have encouraged (and been encouraged by) each other to be real. The bad news is some of those emotions feel pretty lousy at times; the good news is they don't last forever. But then again, neither do the good ones. When we can approach each other (and, God forbid, ourselves) with compassion, those feelings can settle into the appropriate places—neither better nor worse. May you have such a community around you who knows the true-blue you from the inside out.

Which feelings were you told to hide in your life?

How do you remember that feelings aren't facts, and tough seasons always come to an end?

One Verse for Thought:
In the same way, it is better to go to a funeral than a celebration. Why? because death is the end of life's journey, and the living should always take that to heart.
–Ecclesiastes 7:2, VOICE

all that's sacred

For my first several decades of life, I prided myself on being tough. I tried to not need people more than they needed me, never wanting to be indebted. I offered sage advice but never sought it. I was guarded in all my exchanges and rigid in all my opinions. It's a wonder I didn't crack in half every time I sat. When hard times came or relationships ended, my heart endured some bruises but I wouldn't give life the pleasure of knowing it had hurt me. It's almost as though I willed my heart not to break.

There's an old Jewish story that suggests God writes the law on our hearts, so when they do eventually crack, God falls in. I experienced this first when I had a child and developed a major heart fault line. I found I was soft in the worst possible ways—weepy, worried, clueless. I needed help. I needed knowledge. And baby girl didn't give a rip about my opinions. And when my marriage imploded and I looked around for that tough girl in her twenties, I found she'd been replaced by a frightened, mousy woman who was terrified of living.

I marshalled my forces but the fracture deepened.

And finally, when I came back to God and got into counseling and saw the whole of my life to date, my heart shattered with such force I thought there was no way to recover. Only then, though, did it feel like God clapped His hands together and said, "Finally! Now we can get somewhere!!"

When I look back, all that I held sacred—the fearlessness, self-sufficiency, hard-heartedness and self-protection—only prevented me from living fully. I may have been safe, but I also was stunted. Despite the pain and grief and not-knowing, I am so grateful I didn't waste any more years clinging to the illusion of a safe haven. I've come to believe there is no such thing—not for ourselves, not for our children.

If we let it happen, a heart cracked fully open lets us take the whole of life in—all the joy, grief, wonder, adventure, and achievement. Only by dropping our guard do we truly get to *live*.

What do you hold sacred?

In what ways has your broken heart opened you up or shut you down?

ONE VERSE FOR THOUGHT:

I am leaving you with a gift—peace of mind and heart. And the peace I give is a gift the world cannot give. So don't be troubled or afraid. **–John 14:27, NLT**

one less

So often single moms come to our dinners reeling from what feels like the second biggest betrayal: the loss of friends after separation, divorce, or widowhood. Whether from the fear that divorce is contagious to simple cluelessness, losing a close friend can make a wrenching time in our lives that much more isolating. Nearly every single mom I've spoken to has experienced this in the aftermath of her relationship ending, at a time when she most needs support. Then later, when we grow and change and adjust to single parenthood, more friendships can fall by the wayside as we lose common ground and the ability to empathize with each other's lives.

There's no grief like the-loss-of-a-longtime-friend grief. I've known women whose long-time friends cannot relate to their new role as single parent; for those with shaky marriages, the threat may be too close to home. Some lose friends because their schedules no longer allow for much free time. For others, we simply outgrow each other, or learn it was far too one-sided for far too long. Still, each loss carries such a sting that we may be fooled into thinking we should never open ourselves up to deep friendship again.

I've gone through enough of these losses to know that, in the end, God is truly all I have. While this may sound fatalistic, hear me out. Yes, I have dear friends who've been part of my life for decades and whom I cherish. But we need to acknowledge that we *all* can fall short on the friendship front, despite our best intentions. We fail to pick up on needs. We have unmet expectations. We don't have as much time to give each other. We mess up but won't ask for forgiveness or accept grace. In short, we're human. But if we can drop the dream of *any* human person (friend, husband, child) meeting all our needs, and shift our thinking to the One who can, our relationships can get a whole lot better…and our willingness to open up once again after the hurt is an act of wisdom, not foolishness.

In what ways did your friendships change along with your marriage/ partnership status?

How have expectations in your friendships caused difficulties?

ONE VERSE FOR THOUGHT:

Look and see, there is no one at my right hand; no one is concerned for me. I have no refuge; no one cares for my life. I cry to you, Lord; I say, "You are my refuge, my portion in the land of the living." **–Psalm 142:4-5, NIV**

small comfort

I sat next to her as she sobbed, gasping for breath, taking in
the unthinkable. Another school shooting, so much closer to
home at Umpqua Community College in Oregon, with students *her* age killed for no reason. As I took up my well-worn
role as human tissue dispenser, I myself wondered wearily
when, and how, this will all end.

Since that night there've been dozens more tragedies. My
only reaction these days, it seems, is a knowing, grieving sigh.
It's not that I don't care; it's just that I have no shock left, sadly. My heart lives in a state of brokenness and has for years.
This cannot be what He had in mind.

For single moms especially, I think it can feel as though
we have even less protection, that it is only us—only tired,
frightened, alone us—against all that threatens to attack. Just
as there's no handbook on raising children, there's also not
one that deals with raising these kids in a horribly uncertain
world where innocents are gunned down and public events
are bombed hatefully in the name of "love." I have struggled
over the years to first protect entirely, and then guide carefully, my equally tenderhearted daughter through the minefield
that is the evening news, and I wonder whether there's truly
more disaster happening nowadays or we just get to hear
about it, across the globe, 24/7.

I told Em that night, even when there can be no reason,
there can be redemption; if we do not believe that, then our
faith is so hollow as to be blown away in the slightest breeze.
Still, my war-weary heart was remembering C.S. Lewis's
wisdom when he suggested we don't necessarily doubt God

will do the best for us, but rather wonder how painful that best will be. The best, as of late, feels painful indeed.

How do we live in the midst of a world that seems to be imploding? How do we protect and comfort when the unthinkable continues to happen? I do not know, but trust in the promise that things will be made right in due time, and there is still much joy and beauty and grace on the road to eventually. This is not to take away from all the suffering that occurs, but rather to be the ones who coax the hurting ones along, offering a small, safe place to rest amidst the chaos.

How do you reassure your children in the face of tragedy?

In what ways do you let them see you question and struggle yourself?

ONE VERSE FOR THOUGHT:
He will wipe every tear from their eyes, and there will be no more death or sorrow or crying or pain. All these things are gone forever. **–Revelation 21:4, NLT**

giving up

After all these years, I've yet to meet a single mom who said of her former partner, "You know what? We just grew apart." Sadly, I've heard literally hundreds of stories of cheating and drugging, lying and hitting, and usually it's the mom who's holding everything and everyone together, at enormous personal cost, until she simply can't anymore. Then, later, in the silence of starting over, the inner recriminations get louder— if we only tried harder, loved deeper, looked better, maybe it wouldn't have ended. While somewhere deep inside we know how little we had control over, that picture-perfect life still shines brightly in our imaginations.

But what if, instead of beating ourselves up, we could quietly accept the truth: that the illusion of perfection is just that—an illusion? Giving up on a perfect life is worth grieving indeed; we let go of the hope as we also reconcile the impossibility of it ever happening. But it's only over time that we learn what we clung to so tenaciously were also the things that kept us from becoming real.

After all these years, I can finally look back at the end of my marriage as the start of who God made me to be— when I finally gave up the smoke and mirrors for more reality than I could swallow at first. If I hadn't loosened my grip on the prison of perfection, I don't think I'd still be here, in so many ways. And despite the pain and grief and fear, I'd do it all again—ten times over—to have the beautifully imperfect life I have now, the one that holds so much more peace and promise and hope and truth than I could have had back when I was pretending.

Who are you now? Where are you going? And more importantly, who will your children become because you paved the way for them—not to be perfect, but to grow into themselves, imperfectly? Here in the rearview mirror, it seems a small price to pay: What once was a sign of surrender is now the sign of a new beginning.

What has it cost you to give up on the hope and dream of a "perfect" family?

Which qualities are more apparent in the true you versus the pretending you?

ONE VERSE FOR THOUGHT:
Don't revel only in the past, or spend all your time recounting the victories of days gone by. Watch closely: I am preparing something new; it's happening now, even as I speak, and you're about to see it. I am preparing a way through the desert; waters will flow where there had been none.
–Isaiah 43:18-19, VOICE

halved in the sharing

We'd sat next to each other on the sofa, all cried out over our beloved neighbor's death. And again, years later, with silent tears in a rental car following my dad's memorial. More recently, my girl and I have simply lamented the hardness of life together. In America, we're taught that grief should be a short, solitary experience but I cannot think of anything that will make the process longer or harder. These days, I'm far less cautious about letting my daughter see my heart and tears when it comes to grieve-worthy matters because I think they teach her far more than celebrations do.

We single parents have had our fair share of grief, over lives that weren't supposed to be this way, over help that wasn't forthcoming. It's apparent to me, on the frontlines of Eve's Daughters, that many of us (myself included) still carry the shrapnel of some hard relationships. Throw in our kids' challenges and it becomes even more personal. How do we teach them, while reminding ourselves, that life has groaning throughout? And, further, that there's nothing abnormal about it?

We can remember that light is more appreciated after you've stumbled in the dark, and that sometimes we gain everything by giving something away. How people trump stuff any day, and that all we can count on, really, is change. We can share the paradoxes that life reveals now, giving our kids a head start on navigating this wild world.

Part of this entails community. One of the beautiful gifts of our group over the years has been seeing the kids create their own little tribe, sharing their stuff and helping each other along.

It's a hard question, whether the suffering is worth the price to be able to pass along wisdom and compassion. But we're seeing, even in the youngest of our crew, that doing life together has its own banged-up sweetness, that somehow disappointments get halved in the sharing.

In what ways have you healed from your deepest disappointments?

Who are the ones, for both you and your kids, who've helped hold your grief?

ONE VERSE FOR THOUGHT:
The Lord is close to the brokenhearted and saves those who are crushed in spirit. **–Psalm 34:18, NIV**

5

one different angle

ON GAINING PERSPECTIVE,
CHANGING OUR MINDS, AND
LIVING WITH GRATITUDE

girly man

Living outside of Portland, Oregon, we usually have fairly mild winters. But one season produced such a dump of snow that I found myself a little anxious—ironic for a Midwestern girl like myself. Anxiety is a regular occurrence for me when things are out of the norm; power outages, snowdrifts, freezing temps, floods, locusts and plagues set me a little on edge. I find myself hypervigilant during these times, vibrating with efficiency, to protect my daughter from the elements, ensure I keep the home fires burning and stand ready for any emergency. It's just little old me against a whole bunch of bad possibilities.

Some people watch the snow fall, lazily nursing a hot toddy. I spend my time scanning the horizon furtively with an eye tic, thinking of the million ways we could die.

So during our severe weather I had a pipe burst outside, and in the subsequent Three Stooges-esque scramble to get the water main turned off and attend to my circa-1981 water heater, I came to the conclusion that I make a lousy guy. All the guys I know would not have started bawling in frustration as I did after one thing tripped another, from hearing the pipe burst to digging like a retriever in the snow to uncover the main water valve to affording the $175 after-hours plumbing call.

This is the kind of stuff that makes me feel especially alone, even though my former husband was the kind of guy who would have said, "Call a plumber." There is something to be said for having another adult in the area to whom you could comment, "Doesn't this just suck?" And he'd say, "It sure does suck." And you both could eyeball the damage together and agree on the suckitude of the situation.

Once again, it was community to the rescue. My rental husband, Colin, talked me down over the phone and told me what I needed to do in the short-term; girlfriends listened and laughed (after it became funny, which, admittedly, took a while for me) and two men from church came to fix the broken pipe. While I may always remain a girly man, this was yet another example of that graceful balance of asking for help while also getting a glimpse of what we're made of.

How have you handled various emergencies?

What do you think your kids have learned from watching you?

One Verse for Thought:
The Lord is good, a stronghold in the day of trouble, and He knows those who take refuge in Him. **–Nahum 1:7, NASB**

life in the meantime

I bit it big-time yesterday. Sitting through an over-the-top, publically presented, single mom "success story" of redemption and provision and relief, I bought into the Big Lie (or at least one of the Top Ten Big Lies), which is that God loves certain people more than others because He's raining down blessings on them instead of, you know, me. Or, perhaps, you. In this story, people were practically tripping over themselves to help this single mom. She got almost everything she needed or wanted and then some. Oh—and a great new guy, too! I listened while holding my jaw in my lap and thought, "This is not my reality...or the reality of the single moms I know."

Truth is, the story was a set-up. It was intended to look as good as possible. The problem with this, though, is it discounts and discourages the scads of other single parents who are doing the daily slog without all the fireworks and multiple blessings from above. I call this Life in the Meantime (LITM), and it is the life I lead 99.9% of the time. It consists of dog hair tumbleweeds, homework nagging, milk shortages, and medical lab results that suggest I have another something to deal with. It also consists of working closely with other single moms—one who's going through the ringer, one who's doing better, and one who's not sure which end is up or whether she'll surface ever again.

My fabulous new and helpful spouse is apparently on back order. My toilets are dirty. I'm tired but managing.

LITM.

I needed a reminder, so I will do it here, for your benefit as well: LITM is holy work. It's not flashy or glamorous, but it's solid and necessary. It's my church these days...the place where I show up, hoping to hang with God in and around the other stuff, and people who make me laugh, witness my tears, and otherwise cheer me on. It's not neat, tidy, or optimal, but it's incredibly real and rich in its own way.

To survive the success story that was supposed to benefit me, I talked with a friend, cried a little, walked my furry girl, and generally got back to basics. I don't want to cheapen my life, my God, your life, or what we're called to do on behalf of single parents by falling for the Good Life = God's Good Graces deal. It's not only untrue, it dims the honorable work we're called to do, on our own, one day at a time. Know you are building a life for you and your kids that's solid, safe and beautiful—in the meantime.

What are some of the biggest lies you believe?

How do you manage to come back to center?

ONE VERSE FOR THOUGHT:
Send out your light and your truth; let them guide me…
–Psalm 43:3, NLT

the gift of right now

As much as I'd like to think otherwise, I struggle with gratitude. A trillion times I have harrumphed at my present circumstances, thinking they weren't nearly as good as what the beautiful future I envisioned would hold, and so I've missed out on what's right in front of me because my eyes were too busy scanning the horizon. The problem with this, of course, is that when we project into the future, today becomes, by contrast, unremarkable and unappreciated.

When my daughter was a baby, I couldn't wait until she was mobile. When she was mobile, I couldn't wait until she stopped toddling over to the stove to pull the dishtowel down 739 times each day. When she finally stopped pulling the towel down, I couldn't wait until she was old enough to have real conversations. When we could finally have conversations, I couldn't wait until she stopped asking a thousand questions. When she stopped asking a thousand questions, she became a pensive middle schooler.

You see where this is going.

I do not have all the things I've wished for, but I have plenty that I didn't, some of which are actually really, *really* good. I don't have all the answers I'd hoped for, either, but I've learned a few things that have turned out to be more important than I could have known. But every time I run ahead instead of planting myself, taking in the view and exhaling gratitude, I demean those gifts and I demean the Giver.

My guess is each one of you, especially those with younger children, is scanning the horizon for your beautiful future. But I've got to tell you: as time winds down on the parenting front with my girl growing up too fast, there are fewer things

I can't wait for and far more times I want to slow the hours
and appreciate her today.

I wish for you the gift of right now—yes, even the exhaustion, financial upheaval, and unanswerable questions—because the right now will be carried into your future. Make
it sweet.

*What are the things you cannot wait for—the ones that seemingly will
make your life "perfect"?*

How will you choose to live if those things never materialize?

ONE VERSE FOR THOUGHT:
This is the day that the Lord has made; let us rejoice and be
glad in it. **–Psalm 118:24, ESV**

do you see what i see?

I am extremely adept at those "What's Wrong with This Picture?" games. I can usually spot an error from 20 paces, and this ability serves me well in my day job. But sadly, it hobbles me in other areas of my life, when my take on how things are (or how-things-should-be-but-aren't) dims my surroundings just because of my vantage point. I am fabulous at finding what's wrong, and flabby in looking for what's right.

When I was poorer, I thought having more money would solve things. When I've been lonely, I thought having more family, friends, or Mr. Wonderful around would ease it. When I've had health challenges, I believed only the miraculous disappearance of symptoms could heal me.

In art, love, and life, perspective is a tricky thing.

I remember a time when my daughter was thigh-high (versus eye-to-eye, as she is these days), and I was post-divorce and struggling. I really couldn't afford a Christmas tree, but stopped at a lot I drove by each day. The owner pulled out a 7-footer and said, "Can you do $5 for this one? And can I give your daughter a candy cane?" That, to me, is what grace looks like: I couldn't have purchased it with all the money in the world. And my perspective was key, because I could have gone to the place where I wouldn't accept his gift out of embarrassment, where I had to even out the costs and benefits.

Where I'd miss the miracle because I was focused on the wrong thing.

Certain times of the year can be harder for us than others, for many reasons. No one I know is immune from the ache that can come from longing and wishing their picture looked different, least of all me. But I am reminding myself to peer beyond what's in front of me, to change my take on things, to spend the time enjoying my girl because, too soon, she'll be out of the nest.

Always remember: What looks humiliating, hopeless, or humbling now may turn into a treasured memory, a souvenir from the journey…just because you rounded a bend and the light looks different now.

How might you adjust your perspective on someone or something that's causing you pain?

What lessons could you share with your kids about viewing life differently?

ONE VERSE FOR THOUGHT:
Your heart will be where your treasure is.
–Matthew 6:21, GW

thanksgiving

It's been half a lifetime since I spent the holidays with my original family. I was 25 when my parents started the long and fractured process of divorcing. I think if I had only known that last Thanksgiving would be the *last* Thanksgiving, I would have paid more attention.

Not long ago, my favorite aunt passed away. She was the one who always hosted Thanksgiving, who always saved for me the critical job of making the onion dip. The Maker Of The Dip was a position in which I took great pride, because it started before I was tall enough to see the top of the counter and lasted through my young adulthood. When I moved away from Chicago in my thirtieth September, newly married and incredibly homesick, I called her and my uncle that first Thanksgiving and could barely choke out the words: "I wish I was there making the dip."

I think it's human nature to want to go back, to get a do-over, especially when things ended poorly. There was much broken in my family that could not be repaired, at least not in an earthly timeframe. Most of the people I celebrated with all those years ago have passed; others are estranged, with more than just miles between them. During these most wonderful times of the year, I often have a foot planted in the past and future, missing the now. But this present-blindness causes such useless loss. I practice stopping and thinking of the strangers who've become like family, who consider us kin. I think of the care of the C/Kathies, my friend Bonnie's quick, dark wit, Mollie's generosity, Melinda's grace, Alan's conversations, and Colin's and Brian's home repair help. I think of my girl having a way different foundation than I did, by the grace of God, and how her life will be different. I think of what we've built and survived—our little family of two.

So, even as I have the old snapshots scrolling through my head—the black-and-whites of childhood holidays and people long gone—today one of us will be cooking stuffing in our jammas, and one will be eating it for breakfast, also in her jammas, while watching the Macy's parade. We've carved out our own traditions over the years. And I will also silently drink a toast to my aunt Patty, the great trainer of the Dip Maker, and ask to be just slightly more mindful of today. Though I love it, this season can hijack my attention so I focus on what I seemingly don't have.

I'm praying to see what I do.

Which holiday traditions have you carried over to your kids, and which have you left behind?

Whom do you consider "family" these days?

ONE VERSE FOR THOUGHT:
Go back to your homes, and prepare a feast. Bring out the best food and drink you have, and welcome all to your table, especially those who have nothing. This day is special. It is sacred to our Lord. Do not grieve over your past mistakes. Let the Eternal's own joy be your protection!
–Nehemiah 8:10, VOICE

exiting chaos

I am a recovering hyper-committer. I'd love to blame it on my divorce but, the truth is, I was that way long before. Somewhere along the line, I learned all I was good for was working hard, fast and lots, so I said yes to practically everything, and then seethed with resentment. Doing this for a few decades can catch up with a girl. About seven years ago, my health started going—first my thyroid, then my adrenals, then the rest of my stupid endocrine system—and, boy, was I pissed off. It never dawned on me that my plow horse body would give out—*never!*—and it was a shocker of a betrayal. And yet, circumstances forced me to drag my heels through the five stages of grief to land at an uneasy acceptance. I sure wish things were different, but here we are.

I'm learning I function much better in what I call my Zenny place—manageable, organized, quiet. Unfortunately, life as a single mom isn't like that with any regularity, so I have to move toward it purposely. When I have friends over for dinner, I no longer sterilize the house and autoclave the dog prior to their arrival. (Poor dog's already been sterilized.) I'm also learning to get back to reading, which requires one sit still (imagine!), and ignore the sticky notes all over my desk, which are in six different colors (meaning I've gone through six different pads recently). As they say in 12-Step, *Progress, not perfection.*

Someone with some actual perspective reminded me that being a single mom requires a *lot* of juggling. Somehow, I forget, even as my body remembers and screams for me to slow down. But the bigger issue is, for single moms or not, we are prone to over-commitment today. The more we do, the faster we're expected to go; the more technology, the quicker we're supposed to work.

Why?

When I meet with single moms these days, I ask whether they're taking care of themselves, and the answer is almost always *no*. Then I tell them how I blew out some really lovely and useful glands and encourage them to rethink the self-care.

Can we make a pinkie promise to jump off the rat wheel every now and again? You're not only entitled, you must: Too much is riding on it.

How would life look if you didn't have to run so fast?

What steps can you take to slow down and exit chaos?

ONE VERSE FOR THOUGHT:
Come to me, all who are tired from carrying heavy loads, and I will give you rest. **–Matthew 11:28, GW**

the grateful place

In the worst moments of my life, I've talked God's ear off. I've prayed without ceasing as the Bible instructs, but frankly it was mostly for personal benefit. Then, when the crises have passed, I've not been quite so chatty; it's taken years to cultivate a habit of gratitude, of constant communication if only to say thanks.

I believe thankfulness truly is a habit, like flossing; you do it even though you're tired and you'd rather just fall into bed. But even though life has gotten monumentally better in recent years, I've always stopped short of thanking Him for my problems. I have spent more than my fair share of time in 12-Step meetings, and have heard regularly that my life will be transformed as soon as I can start being thankful for my addictions, afflictions, and people who've hurt me deeply.

This is just wrong on so many fronts. Upon considering the potential truth of it, my insides haven't just screamed *no*, but *hell no.* But crazily, I've learned that it's true. It's also true that it sucks, and that it's hard, but somehow once I was able to pray for good things to happen to bad people, life started to get a little lighter.

Paul, the superhero of the New Testament, writes in Philippians that he knows what it is to be in need, and he knows what it's like to have plenty, and he learned the secret of being content in any and every situation. Amazingly, he wrote this from jail, during one of his many imprisonments. He said he can do everything through the One who gives him strength...and I believe part of that strength comes from a grateful place. Regardless. From crisis to calm and back again, gratitude has to remain a constant for true healing.

It can be both brutal and freeing to be grateful for the bad in our lives, but in a weak moment I decided to give it a try. And while I probably should have started with something a little easier, I chose my former husband. Instead of thinking how much better life would have been if we'd never met, or wishing I'd spent just a few lousy minutes contemplating the many red flags early on that became *painfully* obvious in hindsight, I have to be grateful to him at least for helping create an amazing daughter. I cannot imagine my life without her…and I wouldn't have her without him. If that's the only thing I can be grateful for, it is enough.

Look at the long road you've been on, and look at your precious kids: For every detour and pothole, can you give thanks?

What would it look like to be thankful for your challenges?

In which ways could you be grateful for the last person you'd ever forgive?

ONE VERSE FOR THOUGHT:

…give thanks in all circumstances; for this is God's will for you in Christ Jesus. **–1 Thessalonians 5:18, NIV**

running on empty

I am adept at pouring out, but terrible at filling up. Some people think I have everything figured out because of my work at Eve's Daughters. That would be a lie. I still worry about my kid, my money, my job, and my health, just like everyone else. And often, I'm running on fumes and edging on burnout, just like everyone else, too.

Google "parenting burnout" or, even better, "single parent burnout" and you'll see what happens when we don't fill our tanks. Parenting is caregiving, and caregiver statistics are pretty scary, with high levels of stress and illness. When pressed, people in helping professions confide how impossible it feels to fill up before they're asked to pour out again… and I think the same goes for us as single parents.

Sadly, so much about single mom burnout—being isolated, slapping away the hands that could help, shortchanging our sleep, starving our spirits, and striving too much—is just another day, a way of life. I do these things on a regular basis; when it gets to be too much, I go into preservation mode for a while. Still, it would be nice to not have to flame out before actually taking care of myself.

After too many years of running hard and my endocrine system's subsequent fall from grace, I'm learning:

I need quiet time. Note this is not isolating or hiding from life. Instead, it's more time to dream, read, rest, play, connect. This is where you can rely on others for playdates and kid-swaps so you can indeed carve out a little time for yourself.

I need God time. If you're not overly spiritual, it may be time in nature, surrounded by beauty. Whatever it is that gets you centered and anchors your soul, schedule it in.

I need together time. Preferably with others who understand—for me, other single moms, those in non-profit work or the self-employed. Being heard and understood go a long way.

As single parents, we must encourage others and truly listen when they encourage us to fill our tanks. Let it sink in: We pour out so much and make it look effortless but, the truth is, there are only so many miles we can go on fumes. Think about the top three things you need to raise your babies well over the long haul…and fill your tank with those.

Which feelings fuel you as you parent day after day—pride, grit, fear, exhaustion, joy, chaos?

What do you need most to keep balanced and sane during this parenting marathon?

ONE VERSE FOR THOUGHT:
It's useless to rise early and go to bed late, and work your worried fingers to the bone. Don't you know he enjoys giving rest to those he loves? **–Psalm 127:2, MSG**

silencing the voice

We've all had instances of being gutted by people who claimed to be friends or family. The wounds go deep, the resentments build, and often the only solution is geographic—that is, creating space between us and the offender.

But that's so hard to do when the offender lives in your head. Author Kathy Vick writes, "Often the loudest voice in our head is the rantings of a saboteur. I like to refer to her as 'the bad girlfriend' because if she were a real woman I would have nothing to do with her. Unfortunately, she lives inside my mind and took up residence there long ago."

I don't know about you, but I regularly have discussions with people who are not there, manufacturing entire conversations silently, teeming with snarky putdowns and angry protestations on how they done me wrong. (Seriously: I'm at my most witty in my head. You should listen in sometime.) This is the result of one of my many character defects, which is hypersensitivity. I take offense as often as I take in oxygen, as it feels safer to me to feel angry versus hurt. I like to think this practice protects me from the aches of the world but instead it just keeps me stuck in deep, self-created ruts of pain, blame, and martyrdom.

The only thing worse is when the conversations are directed toward *me*, the chiding voice in my head growling like one of those quivery, yappy dogs. It's an unending attack on all the things I've done wrong: how my parenting isn't good enough, my bank account not padded enough, my home not big enough…how foolish it is to trust God with my life and my kid, how there is no truth and no justice, and how no one will ever love me.

The Voice knows how to go for the jugular every time.

I'm so used to the deprecating running dialog I forget to question the veracity of it. What I'm learning is, the way to silence The Voice for good is twofold. First, there's a lot of relief by filtering the commentary through God's Word and focusing on what *He* thinks of me. Second, we bring The Voice out into the world and then hammer it senseless with the obvious truth, which is that we all are doing so much better than we are led to believe. For me, this happens in community, with God, with trusted, *good* girlfriends and with the life-giving phrase *Me, too*.

Let's commit to focusing on the truth—for ourselves, our kids, and each other—and put The Voice on mute, where it belongs.

Which lies about yourself are the easiest to believe?

What would life look like without the negative running commentary?

One Verse for Thought:

Finally, brothers and sisters, whatever is true, whatever is noble, whatever is right, whatever is pure, whatever is lovely, whatever is admirable—if anything is excellent or praiseworthy—think about such things. **–Philippians 4:8, NIV**

last august

I am the mother of a high-school senior. I don't know how this happened—I don't feel 17 years older, until I look in the mirror. This August seems like the last August of a simpler, slower time; I imagine the next year will flow quickly, so I'm forcing myself to stop and remember.

Working with so many single moms in so many situations, I see myself in them all: The ones whose anger propels them out of bed in the morning, and the ones whose tears cannot be stopped. Some struggle, exhausted, chasing a toddler who's recently discovered the world or dealing with an emotional, mouthy teen. The storylines blur until they're essentially one and the same—parenting as best and as hard as we can, until it's time for them to go.

My daughter rolls her eyes these days whenever I start a sentence with "You used to"; she does not wish to go backward. I, on the other hand, seemingly do not want to go forward, stuck in a montage of what-was. She is roaring onward, pulsing like rapids, and it is all I can do to keep my head above the foam and hope that I've raised her well enough.

She is a force of her own accord, yet I know I've etched her indelibly, as she has me. As we have each other. To say I am thankful for the single moms in my life is an understatement because our stories overlap, memory in the making.

We understand where we're coming from and dream of where we want to go. Raising these children together, each stage and every launch becomes a community effort, celebrated by the whole. Between my family, my friends, my single moms, my daughter, and my God, I made it this far, and

I know in my bones I could not have done this alone. May we all have such a tribe of supporters, of stories, of stones upon stones, building us up and carrying us through.

What does life look like on your craziest days?

And what might it look like as an empty nester?

ONE VERSE FOR THOUGHT:
And let us not grow weary of doing good, for in due season we will reap, if we do not give up. **–Galatians 6:9, ESV**

6

one mustard seed

ON SQUELCHING THE DOUBT, SURVIVING THE SILENCE, AND BELIEVING THE INVISIBLE

signposts

Very early on a recent Saturday, my daughter and I were driving to the airport for a 6 am flight. There are two main routes there, one of which I take 99% of the time. At the last second, I decided to take the second, which entailed a bridge being out, and a long reroute, and a hairpin turn to get back on the highway, and so on. Thankfully it was yet the middle of the night, but still: I felt that panic that rises when you can't get your bearings and time is of the essence. This in fact describes much of my life as a single mom: bearingless and racing against the clock.

I am a planner: the more detailed, the better. I meet deviations and reroutes with a set jaw and grim determination. But time and again in my single mom walk, I run into detours that take me off the beaten path and, in my mind, off course. Jobs changing, budgets exploding, illnesses unexpected, misunderstandings abounding: I want to be able to see every turn and avoid every pothole, but often God only shines enough light for my next step.

I cannot think of one of my single mom sisters for whom this is not also true. From notices of eviction to positive biopsies, from loss of custody to the dull soul ache that says something needs to change, we all are off-roading it regularly, scanning the horizon, looking to get back on the expressway as soon as possible.

Ironically, faith—that nebulous, indescribable entity—is the only thing that can serve as compass when we are scared, lost, and fresh out of clever...the kind that's grown in the darkness, when we're groping for anything to keep our balance. His Word says He is there then, when we cannot see, when we're sure of nothing. It takes a leap to believe that when traveling in the shadows...but Who better to guide our way?

I may never stop being a planner or get rid of the control freak tendencies that are like gum on my shoe. But He knows how often you and I will come to the ends of ourselves, and gives us just enough guidance to get on the road again.

How do you react when life throws you a significant detour?

In what ways can you take God at His word that He has good planned for you?

ONE VERSE FOR THOUGHT:
People do their best making plans for their lives, but the Eternal guides each step. **–Proverbs 16:9, VOICE**

on faith

When Cathy and I started planning Eve's Daughters, we talked for hours about how our faith should shape the organization. Both of us came to Christ through crisis; both of us had survived our fair share of judgmental Christians. How could we live our beliefs without scaring (or scarring) those who had a terrible experience with God or His people?

In the time since, we've been criticized for being a "Christian organization" and "not Christian enough." We're not going to win that tug-of-war. What we can do, though, is serve. Many people have asked about our stories, and how we got where we are. Individually and collectively, our stories are of faith and doubt, trial and error. You know, like everyone else's. Maybe that's part of what's making our community grow: Our commonness in inclusive.

In talking with a friend about maintaining our vision while not failing our faith, she reminded me that Jesus met people where they were. For the woman caught in adultery, He met her at the well. For others, He shared a meal (or His heart) or met a need. He didn't demand that these people meet Him at the Sunday service to get His help. And I think this is the closest explanation of what we're hoping to accomplish in our community.

There is *so* much judgment that comes with being a single mom, especially a single-by-choice or divorced mom, in today's society. And, as such, there can be so many strings attached to assistance or acceptance that we remain caught, unable to move forward and do the part of our work that's truly ours to do.

Somewhere along the line we had to make peace with not being all things to all people. Surely this mirrors parenting, the serving and accepting and wondering and knowing our kids won't like us at times. How invaluable to have a community of other moms and kids who can survey the land, plant the seeds, and provide the water for our families when we're absolutely parched. Through it all, hope puts down roots that maybe, just *maybe*, we'll make it through and our kids will be just fine.

But, thankfully, it will never be all because of us.

How do others in your community help parent your children?

In which areas of your life do your "seeds" need water from someone or something else?

ONE VERSE FOR THOUGHT:
Not one of these people, even though their lives of faith were exemplary, got their hands on what was promised. God had a better plan for us: that their faith and our faith would come together to make one completed whole, their lives of faith not complete apart from ours. **–Hebrews 11:39-40, MSG**

trust me

Part of what precipitated my divorce was learning a whole bunch of stuff I never wanted to know. If I came into my marriage seriously lacking in the trust department, I left it completely flattened. It would be easy (and appropriately dramatic) to paraphrase Scarlett O'Hara and say, "With God as my witness, I'll never trust again," but that's a hard, hard way to live.

Raw with remorse and ashamed by failure, I walled myself off, focusing only on my work and my daughter. But that only carried me so far. When life struck yet again, I could no longer stand to be alone: I had to let others in and learn how to trust…even if they'd hurt me.

Little by little, I became more human, meaning I let those pesky needs show, asking for help at times and sharing when I was feeling down. This was my training-wheel trust—requesting and allowing some minor assistance and opening my heart just a tish. Over time, with much practice and some hyperventilation, I went deeper, sharing the journey that brought me here and admitting I did not have all the answers.

The vulnerability that leads to trust, which one friend notes is as comfortable as walking naked around the mall, only threatens us in our own minds. Perhaps it's our hindbrain's way of circling the wagons to keep us safe…but all it really does is keep connection out. I've seen it time and time again in our group: A new mom forces herself to attend a dinner, eyeballing the others furtively and sitting near the door so she can exit quickly. She's worn thin but still of the mindset that she needs to carry this burden alone.

And then she gets pounced on by some understanding but cheery long-timers who love her enough in that moment to encourage her to drop her guard just the tiniest bit and come be part-of.

When we can't will ourselves into trusting, sometimes others can do it for us. All it takes is one step on the road to being known, and God and others will take a thousand more to meet you.

In what ways do you struggle with trust?

What lessons can you learn from your children about putting your hope in the goodness of others?

ONE VERSE FOR THOUGHT:
The Lord is on my side; I will not fear. What can man do to me? **–Psalm 118:6, ESV**

bounty

The night before Em was born, I was having a slight panic attack in the maternity ward. I simply wasn't ready yet. I figured maybe, if she could just be a 15-month baby, I'd be in a better place. I was in over my head and the contractions had barely started; I wondered how in the world I'd ever figure it all out.

I'm not sure I ever did (or will) figure it out, but we have been managing, and now—we're closing in on the high school graduation finish line. I vividly remember our birthing class reuniting and someone saying that our kids would be the class of 2016…and here we are.

I've been surprised lately to find joy in an unexpected place—that of being somewhat overcommitted with Em's crazy schedule. Normally, me and overcommitment, we have a tense détente; it's a necessarily evil in my life. But strangely, I found myself realizing we're in a really good place despite the busyness and the teen years, and this fullness is bringing an unanticipated gift. It took me by surprise to see where we've landed after so many twists and turns; there've been losses and setbacks and dreams that have died, but we've done OK, clinging to faith that we'd make it eventually.

You, too, have had detours you never wanted nor expected. Some of you are grieving big losses, of both people and hope, but still you manage to show up—for work, for kids, for each other—even when you feel there's nothing left to give. The funny thing is that you may end up looking back at this time as a bountiful one, despite what you lack. There's something about the distance that changes our perspective, and in the end it's almost always better to have our hands full than empty.

Come next September, some of you will be hitting milestones with your babies, with some moving up to different schools or going to kindergarten for the first time. You may not be sure how you feel about it but for today, celebrate the bounty—full hands, full heart.

What kind of bounty are you hoping for as you raise your children?

How could your hands be emptier or fuller in this season of life?

ONE VERSE FOR THOUGHT:
And sow fields and plant vineyards, and gather a fruitful harvest. **–Psalm 107:37, NASB**

going out

When I caught up with an old friend, I learned she was taking a trip to scatter the ashes of another friend's mom who died last year. They all were going to Vegas, because that was the mom's favorite place. My friend commented wryly, "Yep, we're taking her home." In the same circle, another friend's mom who was battling a brain tumor when all of us were in our early twenties, told her daughter if she didn't survive the surgery she wanted to be propped up in a cocktail dress at her funeral with her right arm crooked at a 90-degree angle to welcome each person who came by to pay their respects.

I guess we Midwesterners have our own unique thoughts about funerals.

When I think about going out, I remember an assignment in journalism school—writing our own obituaries. I remember sitting, flummoxed, as did all the other students, because we were being asked to predict and record the rest of our (basically) imaginary lives for posterity. And at that age, what did we know about life, anyway? While it may sound like a grim assignment, it helped us focus on how we wanted to live and be remembered.

I am nowhere near as afraid of dying as I once was, which is a wonderful thing. But I also realize that, in the years since J-school, my priorities have shifted greatly. Today, I'd love to learn I actually helped people without my knowing it. I'd love to know a small token given made a huge difference to the recipient. I'd love for my daughter to be able to say, truly and deeply, she knew she was loved with everything I had. And I'd love to know that perhaps someone noticed something in me that was worth a second glance, or a pointed question, of how I lived my life.

It used to be my work that defined me; these days, it's the relationships. I want to carve my name on lives and hearts, leaving memories and legacies for the best of reasons. And, yes, I hope there will come a time when He says, "Good job, you. I knew you could do it."

How does your death help steer your life?

What would you want others to remember most about you?

ONE VERSE FOR THOUGHT:
I am convinced that nothing can ever separate us from God's love which Christ Jesus our Lord shows us. We can't be separated by death or life, by angels or rulers, by anything in the present or anything in the future, by forces or powers in the world above or in the world below, or by anything else in creation. **–Romans 8:38-39, GW**

the desires of your heart

When I first came back to God in the midst of crisis, He was incredibly showy—setting new land-speed records in answering all kinds of prayers and providing for me and my daughter when we had next to nothing. So it felt a little like a bait and switch when, further down the road with Him, my petitions just hung in the air, unanswered. I thought God was mainly in the prayer-answering business; like my amazon. com wish list, I just checked off the items I wanted and let Him at it. So when a lot of my wants—more money, more love, more kids—went unfulfilled, I vacillated between thinking someone didn't give me the magic formula or He was incredibly capricious. Turns out—what a shock!—it was neither. Turns out I just didn't know anything yet about faith.

Hebrews 11 says faith is confidence in what we hope for and assurance about what we do not see. In the long years of being a single parent, I have come to know I can trust God fully; the only sticky wicket is I just can't predict His next moves, which would be incredibly helpful, just saying, in case He's reading this. The assurance I have comes from knowing His character as trustworthy and unchanging through so many miles and trials. But *how* He chooses to answer prayers and grow my faith is anyone's guess. I no longer even try to figure that out.

One of our long-time moms hopes so deeply to remarry and have more children. She's an amazing woman who's been to hell and back over a long number of years, and if anyone deserves a happy ending, it's her. I know better than to say, "There, there" and tell her all will be well, because we've already established that I know next to nothing. But my heart wants to tell her to hold that dream loosely and see what kinds of miracles God has up His sleeve. He may answer her fervent prayer according to factory instructions, or He may take her on the scenic route, changing the view (and perhaps her heart's viewpoint) on the way.

My dear and faithful friend Mollie has reminded me many times that not only will He give us the desires of our hearts (that is, fulfilling our own hopes and wishes and dreams), He will also *place* desires in our hearts toward an end of His choosing. When I look over my journey and see how I came to a place of being something I never wanted to be, working with a population I never wanted to work with, and *flourishing* in the midst, I know it's got to be all Him.

Let go and trust, trust and let go: Your dreams will land in the most benevolent hands.

What are the desires of your heart?

How might it be good if some of those things never came to be?

ONE VERSE FOR THOUGHT:
Delight yourself in the Lord; and He will give you the desires of your heart. **–Psalm 37:4, NASB**

shameless

I was talking recently with a friend about the many surprises that surface when one becomes a single mom. For myself, I was unprepared for the judgment, the shame of having been unable to make my marriage work, and the deep, deep grief of the entire process. She, nearly 20 years older than I, had experienced some of the worst kind of shame—being blamed by her church for not making her husband "happy." There was no support for her there, as there hasn't been for many of you who've found yourselves in similar situations.

We who are single moms by choice, divorce, or abandonment are viewed in a different light than those who are widowed. The truth is, we garner more judgment and less empathy. And when this comes from the church, it stings even worse.

I've tended toward looking at the "orphans and widows" of old to include single moms nowadays, but many disagree...and we can let the judgment of others define us, weighing us down and making the hard job of parenting that much harder. But there is much to be said about a God who turns bad to good, who wastes none of our pain on a transformation we never asked for and now could not imagine living without. There's a strength that comes from knowing we're never forgotten nor overlooked, when we can finally break free from undeserved shame.

Living shamelessly often requires a separation of Church and God (so to speak), meaning we can participate in the messy, clumsy humanity that is "religion" but must focus more on the One who helps keep us going. I confess I came back to God completely broken at age 36, having had little to no use for Him prior. When I realized my own wiliness could no longer save me, it was a humbling moment.

Since then, I've come to believe that He is my first hope for both carrying and ridding myself of the shame, grief, and hurt of feeling forgotten. My second is my community of amazing single moms. When you share your stories, I hear my own, and vice-versa. With each retelling, we become more shameless in the healthiest possible sense.

Do you feel shame or blame over your status as a single parent?

How do you manage those feelings so they don't spill over on others, including your kids?

ONE VERSE FOR THOUGHT:
 So if the Son sets you free, you will be free indeed.
–John 8:36, ESV

good service

Growing up, I cannot recall our family ever volunteering anywhere. I vaguely remember checks at Christmas for "The Needy" but I cannot say I ever met them. Rather, our family prided itself on our self-sufficiency, even from God. To need someone or some sort of help was considered weak, and to be weak was shameful.

I carried this self-sufficiency up to the age of 36, when my daughter was not quite two and my marriage imploded. In some ways, I was well-prepared to be on my own: resourceful, headstrong, and tenacious. But I did not trust well or lean easily, and the God I had just returned to during the crisis of my divorce was asking me to live differently.

First, it seemed I was stripped of my ability to have a self-sufficient life. Somewhat underemployed and without child support, my daughter and I scraped by. But then God arranged for hand-me-downs, and gift cards. I got rental husbands who'd help me with my leaky appliances and shorted wiring. And sometimes God would just cut to the chase and give me cash, through anonymous donors. I would open my mail, see His provision, and cry, a mixture of awe, shame, and relief washing over me.

Through these humbling experiences, I started to serve, first in areas of my proficiency. Still, though, I confess that often my serving had hooks in it—I wanted to look good, helpful, and generous. I wanted to pay back some grace. But in 2007, God told me to work with my friend Cathy to start Eve's Daughters. At that point, I'd slogged through years of single motherhood, but didn't consider myself in any way, shape, or form equipped to help other single moms; in fact, I was terrified to carry out His request. But the crazy guidance from God was to tell these women the truth—that it can be hard and lonely and lean, that you can wonder whether you'll make it. And, while I knew I couldn't promise the hows or whens, from experience I *could* promise that God would show up and be their Husband and Father.

What I've learned in the years since is that, really, I know just this side of nothing and most days God seems pretty happy with that. Through Him, I try to serve now with far less of myself involved. The women I work with don't need all the answers. They just need someone to listen and offer hope. For that, God gave me the gift of mercy in abundance. He has used all of the terrible things in my past, worn down my hard edges, and remodeled me into someone useful in His eyes. But perhaps the biggest surprise is learning that yes, my service helps others, but it also heals me, and the more I am healed, the more I can truly serve.

Time constraints and commitments aside, is there a specific cause or population you've always wanted to serve?

In what ways can you and your kids give back, right where you are?

ONE VERSE FOR THOUGHT:
Whoever brings blessing will be enriched, and one who waters will himself be watered. **–Proverbs 11:25, ESV**

building altars

One of our rock-star single moms approached me at the last community dinner and said, "I have ten weeks left of school." She had tears in her eyes, and rightly so; she's been in school far longer than the many years I've known her, and this particular carrot-on-a-stick has seemed so elusive that sometimes the grief of the waiting has about done her in. This mom has run her own daycare, *started* her school-work around 10 pm every evening, and in a ridiculous twist of grace adopted her former husband's child who was born after their separation, saying she just couldn't let that baby girl grow up in the foster care system. She is, in a word, remarkable.

Money's been tight. Patience and stamina have been tight-er. And here she sits, on the precipice of finishing that degree. Straining to reach the finish line and put the crazy-hard work behind her, she's *so* ready to be done. But I want to tell her to remember: Remember it all…every awful setback and every proud accomplishment, every time you snapped at the kids because of homework looming, and every second they'll be cheering for you 10 weeks hence. Remember Who walked you here.

We single moms can live so scared sometimes, heads down, working hard, that we can't see what God has done for us. *Is* doing for us. I've taken to writing my miracles and provisions down in a journal, simply so I can remember during those times when God seems to have lost my file, when life plays out like that old joke—*He doesn't call, He doesn't write…*

In Old Testament times, people experienced His faithful-ness and built altars—piles of stones, earth, and bricks—as a visual reminder. We need to do the same, to record what we've been through and how we've made it out. It can be something as simple as a beautiful candle, seashell, rock, or other symbol, placed in a small, peaceful place where we can breathe and remember.

For every hard road you've traveled, you've gained souvenirs from the journey, some undoubtedly bittersweet; still, you won't be this way again. Take the whole of it—the smooth paths and the switchbacks, the rains and the winds—and build your own altar, so you and your children will remember.

Do you struggle to remember or forget the hard times you've been through?

How do you celebrate and record the little miracles in your life?

ONE VERSE FOR THOUGHT:
Then Jacob made a vow. "If God is going to be with me, keeping me safe on this journey and giving me bread to eat and clothing to wear so that I return to my father's house in peace, then the Eternal will be my God. And this stone I have made into a pillar will be the first stone laid in God's house…" **–Genesis 28:20-22, VOICE**

everything in season

I had lunch with a friend the other day and we talked about our kids, both in college and approaching the starting line. I told her it's all been such a surprise—from an early wave of grief at the start of my daughter's junior year to the utter excitement I feel for her now as she awaits the results of her first college application.

I look at Em now, in such a good place with her friends and her color guard and her hope for the future, and wish I could get her to see the miracle that got us here. I shared with my friend of getting Em up from a nap when she was not yet two, all warm and waking with a binkie in her mouth, and sitting her on my lap and quietly telling her, "Baby girl? We've got to go. I don't know where, and I don't know how, but we've got to." As I wondered aloud with my friend, would I have left if I'd known then what it would entail? Could I have even fathomed at that time the yet-to-be-developed faith and friendships and provision that would carry us through some awfully lean times?

The liner notes from Amy Grant's song, "It's Better Not to Know," explain that, years ago, Amy and her then-husband planted a number of tiny fruit trees with great hope, tending to them as they did to their fragile marriage, which eventually ended. Decades later, she visited that old farm and learned from the new owner the fate of her trees: The ones that suffered the most from the elements bore the juiciest fruit in the end.

I've spent 21 hard winters in Oregon and the fruit borne—my Emma, my friends, my work—has a sweetness unanticipated. I could not have known. Maybe it's better I didn't.

I know many of you are struggling right now, wondering whether it's been worth it—the hard times, the deep loneliness, the throat-clenching grief. It's true we cannot know going into our decisions what the outcome will be. But I encourage you, as you force those roots deeper every day to raise your babies and protect them and nourish them in ways you were not, that your fruit in the seasons to come will be especially sweet.

How have you learned to keep going in the midst of the unknowable?

In what ways can you look back and appreciate the hard times?

ONE VERSE FOR THOUGHT:
For my thoughts are not your thoughts, neither are your ways my ways, declares the Lord. **–Isaiah 55:8, ESV**

7

one faithful tribe

ON CONNECTING WELL, GOING DEEP, AND DOING LIFE TOGETHER

give a little bit

Some of the most amazing times of faith for single moms come when God mobilizes someone *just* so when we need it most, whether it's a timely call, a meal, a gift card, or an opportunity. And you know how it is: You cry and sigh and blow your nose and think, "OK. Maybe I *can* do another day." The contact is life-giving on a cellular level.

Recently my brilliant and beautiful friend Melinda hatched a simple idea that's taken on Einsteinian proportions. She commits to living her daily life, plus one. That means one extra prayer, one extra sack lunch for someone who needs it, one extra meal, one extra note of encouragement. You know, as moms, a normal battle cry is, "I'M DOING LAUNDRY... DO YOU HAVE ANYTHING YOU WANT TO PUT IN?" So plus one is along those lines, but bigger: If we're doing something anyway, how can we stretch it to help someone else?

Especially in the early crisis days, single moms can feel overwhelmed on a second-by-second basis. I sure did, and then felt guilty on top of it for being so inwardly focused. The truth is, there's a season for each—one to power down and heal, and one to look up and head out from where we landed. Still, there are a million worthy causes and only so many hours in the day. But my friend's M.O. is so...streamlined! As a multi-tasking, recovering-Type A kinda gal, I *love* that in a life-giving, life-changing call to action.

One of my daughter's favorite teachers learned she's expecting, so we packed up a bunch of mom books for her—a few moments and it was done on this end. Will Em's teacher review those books months (or years) from now and remember an unexpected gift that came at an exciting, wondering time?

Sometimes the most simple things are the ones that go exponential…and who knows who you'll impact for the better?

What could plus-one look like at your house?

How could your kids benefit from getting involved in the same?

ONE VERSE FOR THOUGHT:
And don't forget to do good and to share with those in need. These are the sacrifices that please God.
–Hebrews 13:16, NLT

showing how it's done

When Em was born, I was utterly clueless about how to care for her, what to do for her and what to do *with* her. Honestly, if I had been graded those first few weeks (or months), I'm pretty sure I would have flunked. I am eternally grateful for those moms who went before and were willing to share everything they knew about diaper rashes and mastitis, middle-of-the-night feedings and self-soothing (for us, not the babies).

So, why is it that we stop seeking that kind of input as our kids get older? There are few women my age who talk about having a mentor mom in their lives as their children navigate middle school, for example, or deal with puberty or ache for a dad who's MIA when all the other high schoolers have intact families. In these instances and more, a mentor mom can provide invaluable help in demonstrating how to handle changes and challenges, which empower the children to know how as well.

We all need to know women who've lived through some hard times, survived various crises and lived to tell; and who've raised children who are *gainfully employed and living elsewhere*—you know, the things we all hope for. I have had mentors and have been a mentor, and it's life-changing on both fronts. You don't have to be struggling or in crisis to have a mentor, and you don't have to carve out a ton of time for the relationship, either. But with so many of us without families nearby to help us raise our babies well, wouldn't it be great if you had an older, more experienced mom on your side to guide you through the ups and downs of child-rearing?

I've been blessed over the years to have a number of great women in my life—of all ages—who've been especially generous in their advice when asked. Many simply had children earlier than I did so, while we're more like peers, they have already lived through those life experiences and been willing to help me navigate my daughter's every season of growth—from the terrible threes to the mouthy tweens to the sometimes tumultuous teens.

Let's face it—there is no "formal training" for single motherhood. How much better could life be with a mentor who's truly invested in your well-being?

What kind of child-rearing challenges are the most difficult for you?

Who might be able to lend an ear and a hand as you move through various parenting stages?

ONE VERSE FOR THOUGHT:
My child, never forget the things I have taught you. Store my commands in your heart. If you do this, you will live many years, and your life will be satisfying. **–Proverbs 3:1-2, NLT**

joining hands

Locally, we are experiencing a crisis—a woman whose husband left her with five babies to raise. *Five*. She is surrounded right now with friends and family and food and help. She is treading water in that love for now, and it's a beautiful thing to watch, but we all know there are a lot of miles ahead of her. Seeing friends react to her loss, expand to their very tender best and give to her in their ache...this is what I want to see for all single moms and their kids. It's become so clear for me: We need that support whether a woman has been widowed or abandoned, whether she filed or he did, and our kids need to be included, not overlooked.

The truth is, some newly single moms get a tsunami of support while others barely get a drip. I've been impacted on a number of levels by this, both personally and professionally, heart and head. What could life look like if people came together and protected these most vulnerable? This is what the church is supposed to do, at its best, but often that doesn't happen. I've heard gut-wrenching stories of the church blaming, shaming, and turning its back on so many single parents. Some of the worst stories I've heard came from women who were formerly married to *pastors*. I only half-joke that somewhere Jesus is putting His fist through some drywall over the sorry state of affairs. It's not supposed to be this way...but maybe we can be part of the change.

Sadly, it seems most of us haven't experienced a taste of this kind of redemptive, supportive, and encouraging community, even in our darkest times, when we've been absolutely parched for it. How do we fix that—so that being alone in our abandonment or betrayal or shame is the exception and not the rule?

Simply, we create that kind of community ourselves, raising our kids in the midst of it, instead of on the outskirts. With purpose, intention, and tenacious hearts, we can bring up these babies in community—equal to, not less-than. Where they belong.

Have you and your kids been surrounded by support or left to fend for yourselves?

What might a community-wide safety net look like in your neighborhood?

ONE VERSE FOR THOUGHT:
Stand up for the poor and the orphan; advocate for the rights of the afflicted and those in need. **–Psalm 82:3, VOICE**

where we left off

I have been blessed with some of the finest women friends available—some long-term, some for a season—and all of them have somehow kept me tethered while encouraging me to go both deep and high. While in Chicago for my dad's memorial service, I was able to catch up with four of my bestest high school girlfriends. It was fabulous because these amazing women—some of whom I knew in junior high—hold parts of my history no one else knows. So in addition to being reminded of incredibly embarrassing things we did, we were able to catch up seamlessly and it felt like we never missed a beat.

In and around some abysmally poor service from a wait-ress who—how shall we say?—was not operating within her area of gifting, we got to spend a few blissful hours laughing, remembering, and encouraging with a side order of some good-hearted mocking. Who knew we'd end up where we are: a long-term married with college kids, a married ER nurse with two adopted kids, a newer mom with two young girls at home, a professional without kids, and a single mom? We've worked, we haven't; we've fought and made up; we've had kids, we didn't; we've had relationships, we've been sin-gle...You'd think we wouldn't have much in common, but you'd be wrong.

And with one who couldn't hear as well, two sharing read-er glasses to scan the menu, most stretching to relieve some stiffness, and a couple saying how this whole aging thing snuck up on us, we were a funny bunch of broads, if I do say.

These are some of the finest friends money can buy, and they have anchored me seemingly for a million years. There's no telling where I might have landed if I didn't know—really, truly know in my bones—they would be there for me, long-term. We all can go crazy amounts of time without talking and pick up where we left off. And *that* is an amazing gift.

Who are the most precious ones who keep you tethered in life?

What can you say to them today to let them know the gift they are?

ONE VERSE FOR THOUGHT:
As iron sharpens iron, so a friend sharpens a friend.
–Proverbs 27:17, NLT

who do you think you are?

Writer Cadence Turpin wrote a great blog post about a shift from doing to being when it comes to introducing people. So, instead of saying someone is in marketing, you'd say she's awesome in a crisis and has a wicked sense of humor. I love this approach, because some of my most amazing friends would demur that what they do isn't important. In particular, my friend Melinda is a more-than-full-time caregiver to multiple family members. I know she can feel like her days are swallowed up with driving to doctor's visits, completing paperwork, and soothing those she loves. But when I tell people about Melinda, I say she is, by far, one of those most insightful, faithful women I know, with an infectious laugh and a love of beauty. And talk about awesome in a crisis… she has had more than her fair share and helps others face challenges with great dignity, humor, and hope.

This process of focusing on who we are versus what we do made me think about our kids as well. I shared with Em recently what I thought were some of my (many) parenting mistakes, one of which was innocently yet publicly describing her as shy when she was younger which, as you might imagine, tended to reinforce her silence. *Shy* is one way of saying it, but I also could have said she's an observer who mulls over things before speaking, which is also quite true; that girl is a deep pool of water. One depiction sounds like a handicap; the other sounds like a gift.

In general, I don't like to spin things and could never refer to a petite person as "vertically challenged" without chuckling, but I like the idea of touting individuals' unique and impressive qualities versus their work. In our communities, we (and our kids) are so much more than what we do; let's focus on the human connection and celebrate what we *are*.

What are three "being" words you'd use to describe your kids?

How would someone describe who you are, instead of what you do?

ONE VERSE FOR THOUGHT:
I praise you, for I am fearfully and wonderfully made. Wonderful are your works; my soul knows it very well.
–Psalm 139:14, ESV

glorious rentals

I saw a piece on the local news about Grannies for Rent—single, older women who don't have any family around "adopt" the kids of single moms who don't have any grandparents handy. So, they spoil the kids rotten, spend holidays with them, develop relationships with the single parent family/extended family, and do life together. Sadly, the story came over the wires from *Poland*. But they are so on to something over there, something needed the world over.

In our lives, Em and I have had a major shortage of grandpas but a plethora of grandmas. I don't recall who said hello the first time, but somehow our amazing neighbors Sharon and Marge took us under their wings, bringing cookies and trinkets and care. They made me recall my own grandmother who, by her own admission, made a far better grandma than mom after she'd mellowed with age. She was the one who took me to Disney movie openings and Big Boy's for a hamburger afterwards. She sewed me a new dress every holiday and kept me at her place when I was sick. She was the one who told my mother (my *mother!*) to lighten up when it came to being fashionable in the 1970s and reminded her that grades weren't everything. Plus, with her farming background, she also could practically field dress a deer, so that was pretty cool, too.

She died around the time I first learned I was pregnant, and some of the sadness I felt in her passing was in the not-meeting; she and Em would've gotten a kick out of each other. Then, when Sharon passed, it was especially hard because that kind of adoration—the kind with no strings attached—is beautiful and rare.

The thing is, our kids need this kind of attention and love, yet so few of us are near biological family these days...and sometimes, our biological families aren't interested in that kind of relationship. But what about, for example, the young-ish widow who has a lot of time and love and talent and chocolate chip cookies to give? Throughout your places of worship, schools and community centers, there are awe-in-spiring seniors who have so much to give and simply want to connect, and the only gift required is your own sweet family.

What kind of relationships do your kids have with older adults?

How could you bring a rental grandma/grandpa into the mix to benefit everyone involved?

ONE VERSE FOR THOUGHT:
Grandchildren are the crowning glory of the aged; parents are the pride of their children. **–Proverbs 17:6, NLT**

come together

Pastor and author Timothy Keller tells of meeting a Bosnian man in New York City sometime around a political election. The Bosnian noted how the Democrats hated the Republicans and vice versa. But while he called himself a strong Democrat, he considered himself a Bosnian first. So, even if he met a Bosnian who was a strong Republican, it was inconsequential to him because, as Bosnians, they'd already experienced life and death together.

One definition of *community* is "a group of individuals who've been bonded into a body through an intense common experience." People who wouldn't normally care about each other can develop bonds thicker than blood due to a shared history. And isn't that what we hope for as single moms? Our "intense common experience" (solo parenting) cements our community—whether divorced, widowed, abandoned, single by choice, it doesn't matter. You need to have a place where you belong.

We recently had an occurrence that had an amazing outcome for a single mom who needed a mentor for her teenaged son. As I wondered where to start, a name popped into my head…a man I knew (barely) from church. Following that lead, I wrote him and, long story short, he indeed agreed to mentor this young man. But the more stunning revelation was that this gentleman's family had already met this single mom and her family months earlier through a different shared experience. She likely wouldn't have thought to contact him on her own, so God arranged it just so for our community to expand just a little more. They connected on a parental level, and everyone benefited from it.

The loneliness of solo parenting can be soul killing, but it doesn't have to be that way. As a community, let's open our arms to ensure all who might benefit are invited, included, and involved.

Which people make up the strongest parts of your community?

Who might be on the outside looking in, needing a gentle invitation from you?

ONE VERSE FOR THOUGHT:
Therefore welcome one another as Christ has welcomed you, for the glory of God. **–Romans 15:7, ESV**

you are here

I had an interesting conversation recently about how churches often scramble to get as many people as possible through their doors but often fail to do the even-harder work of helping those people get as whole (and holy) as possible. My friend said, "Yeah, it's like shoving people through the gates at Disneyland without providing a map to the good stuff inside."

In times of confusion, crisis, introspection, grief, even joy, it seems we need to anchor ourselves in relation to the landmarks around us: God, friends, family, work, kids, hobbies... whatever it is that keeps our footing sure. We are in unknown territory, but that almost always seems to lead to something remarkable. We'll find our way, yet our maps vary, as each of our landmarks and journeys is deeply personal...but all of them have the spot with the X that says YOU ARE HERE.

When I finally moved out of our family home just after my daughter turned three, I was quite proud to have purchased a townhouse for us. It was a total armpit, requiring renovation from top to bottom, but I still vividly recall moving day, barely able to move without shrieking in pain, but getting down on my arthritic knees to thank God for providing this X on the map. I didn't know how long we'd be there but I knew it was a place that was safe, without secrets, and with peace abounding—regardless of the orange curtains, Brady Bunch wallpaper, and avocado carpeting.

As the years have passed, it has become a mission of mine to help develop a community in which X marks the safe, nurturing place for single moms—where a woman can know without a shadow of a doubt that she can learn to do the single mother gig with strength, grace, humor, and health.

I don't want to simply build our numbers, having women streaming through our doors, without a map to what's inside. But the irony here is that our maps can't show a list of directions to follow; rather, they're created over time, individually, step by step, conversation by conversation, friendship by friendship.

When it seems like you've lost your direction, what keeps you anchored?

Where is your safe spot—your X on the map?

ONE VERSE FOR THOUGHT:

We must also consider how to encourage each other to show love and to do good things. We should not stop gathering together with other believers, as some of you are doing. Instead, we must continue to encourage each other even moreas we see the day of the Lord coming. **–Hebrews 10:24-25, GW**

lighting the way

In the past several years, there've been a number of female college graduates in our circle. While I'm always excited for them, I also remember myself at that age…a little lost, fairly terrified, and unsure of my footing. What did I know about the working world?

Back then, during a mandatory summer internship with a local health department, I met Coral, who very nicely told me my first writing assignment made a lovely term paper but wasn't going to cut it in the newspapers. She gave me a formula for feature stories I still use to this day, and praised me up and down when my rewritten piece hit the local papers and I got my first byline.

Some thirty years later, I still remember her.

Coral, my Council of C/Kathies, various pastors and more have served as my mentors over the years, teaching me how to do life. Do you remember the terror of bringing your first child home and feeling like you knew *nothing*? Have you ever been utterly lost in your work or your faith walk, and someone *just happens* to come alongside to help you keep your job and your sanity?

If I hadn't had my mentors, I don't know where I would be…but I certainly wouldn't be *here*. This is why I feel so very strongly about this type of teaching, be it elder-to-younger or peer-to-peer, especially for single moms who are feeling isolated without family nearby. It used to be we had grandmas and moms and aunties helping us raise our kids, but today we are scattered. And the truth is, you don't know what you don't know. Mentoring helps open our eyes, gives us direction, and provides light on our paths.

It's been said you can't keep what you have until you give it away. You have knowledge and experience others need; they have the same for you. Is your kid giving you fits? You're not the only one. Need help polishing your resume? Someone can help. Have questions about your faith walk? There's another who's made that journey before you.

For as much as we pour into our kids, we need to have our tanks filled as well; why not reach out and ask?

In which areas do you feel most lost and in need of support?

How could your kids benefit from having a mentor?

One Verse for Thought:
Instruct the wise, and they will be even wiser. Teach the righteous, and they will learn even more. **–Proverbs 9:9, NLT**

less-than

I still can feel my face burning. A coworker, unaware I was behind her, snorted and said, "I would *never* let strangers raise my children. I'm not one of *those* people!" Seeing as I'd just rushed in from dropping Em at daycare, it hit me: No matter how hard I was working to keep everything balanced, I could not be a good mom in this woman's eyes.

I believe yesteryear's widows and orphans now include today's single moms, but there sure can be a lot more judgment when you're divorced, abandoned, or a single mom by choice. For those of us who regularly feel less-than, shame adds fuel to the fire. The irony, though, is we all have our baseline of what's acceptable and what's not. Just fill in the blank: "At least I'm not _____ !" (What? Poor? Alcoholic? Divorced? Obese?) Over the years, I've heard all kinds of statements that pointedly separate *us* from *them*.

At least I'm still married…

At least I stay at home with my children and raise them right…

At least my husband would never have an affair…

In her excellent book, **I Thought It Was Just Me**, shame researcher Brené Brown suggests one of the biggest things that can help us overcome shame is putting our name and face in the "them" category; that is, realizing each one of us is just one bad decision or one bit of bad luck away from being the very same ones we judge. How easy is it to *tsk-tsk* when we see a woman ignoring an unruly child? Would it help if we knew she's completely burned out from taking care of her terminally ill father? Could we imagine ourselves in her place and finally practice empathy then, instead of standing in ignorant judgment and proclaiming her less-than?

The way through the shame is transparent, supportive, transformative community. There's a great 12-Step saying: You can't heal your sick mind with your sick mind. In the same manner, you can't heal your loneliness and shame while being alone and drowning in it. A counselor once told me we can never really know ourselves until we're reflected back by others, so we need to choose those "mirrors" carefully. Your single mom community reflects your potential, grows your hope, and accepts you as you are, all in a place safe enough to share your stories, unload the guilt and shame, and leave lighter than when you arrived.

Together, we are greater than we can imagine.

In which areas and circumstances of your life do you harbor shame?

How do you help your kids when they feel less-than?

ONE VERSE FOR THOUGHT:
Do not be afraid; you will not be put to shame. Do not fear disgrace; you will not be humiliated. You will forget the shame of your youth and remember no more the reproach of your widowhood. **–Isaiah 54:4; NIV**

8

one dab of tenacity

ON ACCEPTING WHAT IS,
SAYING YES TO WHAT MIGHT BE, AND
HANGING ON UNTIL TOMORROW

what will they remember?

My friend Janet shared an eye-opening exercise with me recently. Working with middle schoolers, she asked them to write down things their moms said to them regularly, and some funny momisms came to light. Janet also explained the sayings noted by more than one person were deleted, so all that remained were the rarer ones.

Here's the surprise: Of all those children and all those sayings, only one teen wrote *I love you* as something he remembered his mom saying often.

Shocked, I asked my daughter when I returned home to list the top ten things she remembers me saying through the years. Then, I braced myself as she handed me the list. Some were especially poignant and some were inside jokes, but I was really thankful she listed #1 as *I love you* and #10 as *I'm sorry*. I was seriously afraid that *HURRY UUUUUPPPPP!* was going to land in the #1 position or, worse, *What were you thinking?*

It was a good reminder about the power of words and, especially, the power of apologies when we get those words wrong. Lord knows, I have hurtled more harsh ones than I care to remember. But the exercise was valuable in recognizing what *did* sink in throughout these long years of parenting, if we keep at it, even when we fail. I know I'm not alone in thinking, "Are you even listening to me?" As Janet observed, our kids take in more than we know—and, thankfully, that includes more good as well.

I've had some anxiety lately that the window through which to shove as much life knowledge as possible is closing—that I'm running out of time with my girl. But maybe more is not better: Perhaps I just need to choose my words more carefully instead of just choosing more words as she gets ready to go into the world.

What do you remember your parents saying to you when you were young?

What do you hope your kids will remember?

ONE VERSE FOR THOUGHT:
Careless words stab like a sword, but the words of wise people bring healing. **–Proverbs 12:18, GW**

things no one ever told me

When Emma was little, we had a little game we played when I wanted to impart some sort of life information. I'd say, "Girlie Tip #1,163: Never wear dark stockings with light shoes" or "Girlie Tip #517: Always write thank-you notes." Now that she's older, I can tell her what I've been trying to do—impart all the things no one ever told me about life, a.k.a., Stuff You Need To Know So Things Go More Smoothly For You.

When I think back, so much of my fear (and subsequent attempts at control) stemmed from the fact that I felt utterly clueless about being in the world—how to act, what others needed, why things were the way they were. For all I learned about keeping house and being on time and working hard and doing algebra, it seems little was divulged about how to actually *live* in this confusing, adult world.

What could happen if we, in age-appropriate ways, regularly shared with our kids the things no one ever told us? That some of their relationships are going to end. Badly. That people who should never leave them or stop loving them will, and they will feel like the bottom of the earth dropped out and they'll never, ever recover. Except they will. That it's not only healthy but normal to grieve, for as long as it takes, life's huge losses. That forgiveness is critical to our mental, physical, and spiritual health, especially when it's not deserved. That no one got **The Manual On How To Live**—not even the beautiful, popular people; we are all just making it up as we go. And, oh Lord…that all of us are trying just as hard as we know how, and when we're tempted to judge and snap "Why is s/he being so *horrible*?", that is the time we must be more tender than we think is possible.

We had to learn all these things by trial and error and by simply hanging on. But what if, in and around the Common Core learning and the science fair projects, we could sneak in a few life lessons of our own to our precious kids? How much further along could they be? Remarkable things can happen when you sit with your darlings and share your beautiful, messy humanness with them via your own family's version of Stuff You Need To Know.

They need to know we didn't always know everything. And we need to remember they never expected us to.

In what ways could you share some of your harder life lessons with your kids?

What do you want your children to know most about managing life?

ONE VERSE FOR THOUGHT:
Place these words on your hearts. Get them deep inside you. Tie them on your hands and foreheads as a reminder. Teach them to your children. Talk about them wherever you are, sitting at home or walking in the street; talk about them from the time you get up in the morning until you fall into bed at night. Inscribe them on the doorposts and gates of your cities so that you'll live a long time, and your children with you, on the soil that God promised to give your ancestors for as long as there is a sky over the Earth.
–Deuteronomy 11:18-21, MSG

the business of reality

I got a call before 7 am on my cell from the boss-lady of my largest writing account. When that happens, I know something has gone terribly awry. Not one, but two last-minute projects blew up my day—the day I had all other kinds of things scheduled. Then, more niggling, obnoxious things that go wrong at bad times occurred, such as the kitchen faucet screen coming loose enough to spray water like a clown with seltzer all over me and my windows.

While wiping up that mess, I cradled the phone on my shoulder and called a young woman with whom I was to meet—a single mom who's struggling. She asked apologetically if we could reschedule. I mouthed *thankyaJesus* as I now had a little more time to put out all the newly erupted fires. I'm not in a position to be turning down paying work; as a freelancer, you have to take it as it comes, but sometimes it comes at the cost of schedule and creativity. I wish I could commit to working for God instead of working for money, but I'm telling you: There are times I wished He paid better.

You know firsthand that reality kind of bites sometimes, edging out creativity, silencing the yearning to do good, and stirring up anxiety. We strive to do what we're called to do—raising kids well, working so we can live, keeping home and hearth going—and then life gets in the way, threatening to derail our best efforts. When this happens, I try to get centered by praying, getting out of my own way, and not giving myself too much credit—like I'm so terribly important the world *might* just spin off its axis without me. (It's possible... but doubtful.)

The reality is, it will all keep going—the work, the parenting, the non-profit and more—with or without me. Better a less accomplished but saner me than the alternative.

How do you react when life goes a little haywire?

Which responsibilities are truly yours…and how many could be handled by others?

ONE VERSE FOR THOUGHT:
Never worry about anything. But in every situation let God know what you need in prayers and requests while giving thanks. Then God's peace, which goes beyond anything we can imagine, will guard your thoughts and emotions through Christ Jesus. **–Philippians 4:6-7, GW**

the tiny life

I have long been of the mindset that more is better, so I tend toward thinking there always must be something bigger to be had, bigger to be done, bigger just in general. All the searching for bigness makes me lose the ability to see the beauty of the small, the precious, the tenacious…but the single parent walk is nothing if not little bits of tiny strung together.

When I was first separated, a day in which I took a shower was a big win for me; it was all I could do to put one foot in front of the other. Even though the divorce was necessary, it was also incredibly wrenching, as I truly longed for a different ending and hoped desperately I wasn't leaving five minutes before the miracle happened. During those dark days, I launched a lot of grocery list prayers (*need help/don't forget/ please hear*), and every day I kept moving and upright was considered a success.

I can look back on that time with some actual fondness now. Great grief and crisis can only be handled in tiny bites, and never have I felt closer to God than during those long and arduous years. Something small encouraged me to hang on, laying the foundation of my spiritual life stone by stone, every choice adding strata until my house was built.

Over time, I've also been afforded the privilege of seeing changes in the single moms I know, seemingly imperceptible at first, then gaining focus. The shift from being in crisis to just past crisis is huge. Then come the choices: to move, return to school, stay single, get remarried, switch careers and more. All of these decisions are made in tiny increments, but I've come to see that small steps eventually do add up to something amazing.

I hope to keep the perspective I crave—that bigger is not necessary better and that my life and the lives of our Eve's Daughters moms were supposed to be this way, a little bread-crumb trail to sustain us, living the tiny life in a big, big way.

In what ways does your life seem small?

How can you envision your perspective changing in the next year, five years, or more?

ONE VERSE FOR THOUGHT:
Stand firm, and you will win life. **–Luke 21:19, NIV**

but what about me?

Years ago when I worked for a large non-profit, my boss, due to her talents and reputation, was asked to coordinate the opening ceremonies of the local Special Olympics. Everything was scheduled within an inch of its life and was going incredibly well until the second-to-last runner decided *he* wanted to be the one to light the Flame. As luck would have it, this young man was extraordinarily fleet of foot, and he quickly bypassed his successor on his way to the platform, torch in hand. When the final athlete realized what was happening, he took off after his predecessor with a vengeance. The race-before-the-race continued out the stadium, and the final runner, from whom glory was snatched, began to cry. What started as something reverent devolved into a lightless, flameless kickoff at which the athletes gaped in amazement and the audience stifled its laughter.

When I heard this story, I laughed...because I recognized how much I'm like the runaway runner: There's a dank, ratty little neighborhood inside me whose residents clamor for attention, want to be highly visible, and will attempt most anything to get what they want when they want it.

This is not a good set-up for your average single parent. In fact, there may be no other situation in which we feel more invisible, forgotten, and put by the wayside. While I hate the needy, prideful part of me, I can't deny it's there. And we cannot expect our ingrate offspring to notice, appreciate, and take care of our mental states because they, too, want what they want and expect us to notice, appreciate, and take care of *them* (and rightly so). It's not a crime to want to be seen; we just need to choose our audiences carefully. When we are desperate for a little applause and a few nods of understanding, we need to go to a well with some actual water in it. This is why we cherish our single parent friends; they truly hear us and validate that ache for what we don't have while cheering us on toward a far-off finish line.

Who can you call for support when you're feeling invisible?

What do you do with your unanswered wants?

ONE VERSE FOR THOUGHT:
The Lord is the one who goes ahead of you; He will be with you. He will not fail you or forsake you. Do not fear or be dismayed. **–Deuteronomy 31:8, NASB**

the weight of being an anchor

There are some mornings in this child-rearing gig when I well up and really am thankful for the job. You know, the sweet moments of crayon drawings and early snuggles, homemade gifts and coupon books. Then there are some mornings when, simply to cope, I feel compelled to shove down maybe a dozen deep-fried apple fritters followed by a pint of Ben & Jerry's Cheesecake Brownie. But this would not be a great thing for my daughter to witness; I'm pretty sure it's the wrong kind of teachable moment.

Here's the truth: Doing the right thing day in and day out is tiring, unglamorous, and highly overrated, yet that's what we single moms keep choosing to do. Of course we want our kids to see and know they can depend on us, but I confess I sometimes get weary of being The Anchor—you know, the one who keeps everything level and safe and, well, *anchored*.

Sometimes it hits me that anchors live a life of unseen servitude while nestled silently in centuries' worth of fish dung. Or maybe that's just how it feels some mornings.

The long journey of trying to raise our kids to be fit to roam the world someday is filled with potholes, switchbacks, and precipices. And, if you're a divorced mom trying to co-parent, you can also find yourself facing seemingly untenable dead ends. It is brutally hard, day after day, to be the one who toes the line, follows the schedule, makes the rules, and keeps everyone's lives in order. Seriously: It can make a girl go on a sugar binge.

While I have too much work to do to make a fritter run (and I'm sure my butt will thank me later), I *am* trying to remember my Lamaze breathing and tell myself we're making great progress on this very large and important assignment of getting someone raised right. The truth is, it really is a gift she knows her mom is an anchor for her.

Maybe the view from the ocean floor will look a little more promising tomorrow.

What does it look like for you to be an anchor for your kids—regardless of what's happening around you?

Who is your anchor?

ONE VERSE FOR THOUGHT:
Consider it pure joy, my brothers and sisters, whenever you face trials of many kinds, because you know that the testing of your faith produces perseverance. Let perseverance finish its work so that you may be mature and complete, not lacking anything. **–James 1:2-4, NIV**

beyond the cape

Pastor and author Steve Wiens recently wrote about a kind of courage that seems overdone—one that wears masks and capes and makes grandiose promises to hide what's lacking. He believes real courage, the kind that comes from a solid and growing place, is actually much quieter.

Recently I returned from Chicago, visiting old friends and old stomping grounds, with a profound thought: My life is full of amazingly gifted women who experience something terrifying on a regular basis and continue to move forward in spite of it. (This is what life looks like, yes?) One just finished a medical mission trip that rocked her world. Some are asking the hard questions about the cost of following their dreams, and others are involved in truly heroic parenting. And my own mom, who's wondered long whether she can hold her own, took a deep breath, submitted her artwork and won two awards.

In seasons of change, we're mostly blind to the amounts of courage and character we actually possess. But while there's no doubt change can be tough, often we find we can be tougher than we'd have imagined. Wiens writes, "Courage is saying yes to what compels you even though you are afraid you don't have what it takes…You'll find that kind of courage when living behind your mask and your cape and your grandiose promises becomes so exhausting that you just can't do it anymore."

These women could have simply stayed stagnant and safe but, once set into motion, they're going places they never imagined. The same is true for you, lovely single mamas. Almost every day, I get to talk with women who cannot see the strength they possess or the God who watches over them. They don't have enough money, resources, or hands to go around. They desperately want their children to have a better life…and even recognize those times when they themselves stand in the way of that. But they are moving homes, moving jobs, moving mountains, and moving on. Just like you.

Choose to live life unmasked and see: The view is amazing.

What choices have you made in life that initially felt terrifying?

What have you gained from making those decisions?

ONE VERSE FOR THOUGHT:
So be strong and courageous, all you who put your hope in the Lord! **–Psalm 31:24, NLT**

showing up

In our household, we've had many talks over the years about doing the next right thing for someone else, even when you don't feel like it. That may mean doing a task you'd rather not, or visiting someone in the hospital even though it freaks you out. With kids, it's hard to express (without crushing their little spirits) that being an adult is not nearly as glamorous as it appears, but these kinds of life tasks really spell it out clearly.

Writer Deirdre Sullivan recalls her father telling her, "Always go to the funeral," meaning people should do the things that inconvenience them a little but mean a whole lot to others. Oftentimes it seems easier on so many levels to just do nothing—to not call the woman whose sister just died, to not invite the new mom over for coffee. But every time we make an inward excuse, we magnify the miles between us in our relationships. Yes, it's hard to put ourselves in those uncomfortable circumstances; it's harder still to be in them alone.

On a recent Saturday night, a single mom's father passed away. How I wished I had a magic wand to either bring him back or ease the pain. Instead, I asked if she wanted to sit together at church the next day, knowing it was likely going to be a tough morning. That's because I was remembering my own father dying early on a Sunday, and sitting with a friend at church because I didn't know what else to do or where else to go. Back then, I leaked through the entire service and Rebecca just kept doing the next right thing—handing me tissues and sitting in silent support—even though it was damp and awkward and terribly sad. What a gift it was just to have her presence.

With the crazy lives we lead and schedules we keep, how important is it to show up, despite the inconvenience? In the end, Sullivan most remembers looking at the rows of people who sat at her father's funeral on a cold Wednesday to pay their respects and show their support. All inconvenienced; all irreplaceable.

I'll bet there are plenty in your circle who need a small gift from you—a word of encouragement, a call to hope, a listening ear. You will need these yourself someday. Maybe even today.

How can you tell the people who've routinely supported you how important they are?

In which ways are you teaching your kids to show up for others by demonstrating it yourself?

ONE VERSE FOR THOUGHT:
Do not withhold good from those to whom it is due, when it is in your power to act. **–Proverbs 3:27, NIV**

latch on to the affirmative

My friend Vibeke is a faithful, compassionate woman with a wicked sense of humor and wisdom that comes from surviving some hard knocks. She's also an awesome mom to three amazing teens and I've turned to her more than once for advice. One of the things I most appreciate about her is her willingness to say *yes*; if potential failure scares her, she surely doesn't show it. And as someone who plans for every contingency, I aspire to be more like her, because I often say a timid *maybe* when I should be saying a joyful *yes*.

When Em was younger, Vibeke turned me onto the idea of Yes Day, for which a budget is set and the answer to (almost) every question is *yes*. While requests need to stay this side of moral, legal, and feasible, it's a fun process to go through. You may find yourselves eating ice cream for breakfast, driving to the coast for lunch, and searching for the swimming pool with the tallest slide at dinner, but it will provide an adventure and another great set of memories.

As my girl gets older, though, the questions become bigger and the yesses become scarier (as in, *Can I take a gap year in Japan?*). I am a hypersensitive introvert with health challenges; sometimes saying *no* is just a lot easier. I don't have to put myself out there, experience any discomfort, or disrupt my routine. But frankly, I don't necessarily want Em to follow my lead here: I remember being her age—hope-filled, excited, and bulletproof—and parental *yesses* are life-giving. Even more so, she needs the practice of saying yes herself to figure out who and what she's going to be in the world without her old, decrepit mother around.

What better gift can we give as single moms than to instill that confidence in our kids and let them know, as their biggest cheerleaders, we have confidence in them to go forth bravely?

When was the last time you said yes with no strings attached?

How do you balance yesses and nos in your household?

ONE VERSE FOR THOUGHT:
For God has not given us a spirit of timidity, but of power and love and discipline. **–2 Timothy 1:7, NASB**

what does your saturday look like?

I had a great series of conversations recently with someone who's been helping me walk through some disappointments. While this person is definitely pro-Karen, he can't walk the path for me. All he can do is listen, point me back to True North, and help me on my journey.

The older I get, the more I suck at waiting. I thought it would be different by now, but I'm the one sighing heavily in the 10-items-or-less lane and fitting in something industrious when a company puts my call on hold. But I have experienced that life as a single parent, for all the work it involves, also entails a ton of waiting: for things to get better, for things to get worse, for things to stop, or start, and so much more.

In my single mom life, I've learned that between a promise ending on Good Friday and a promise anew on Easter Sunday, one can have a long, lonely, questionable, faith-trying Saturday. That's where I'm at right now, on a number of fronts. And you can't always expect people to be willing to hang with you on a Saturday, if you know what I mean: Sometimes, there's other stuff to do, and maybe they're living in Monday or Thursday mode. Saturday friends are truly a gift.

If I rally a bit of faith, though, I know I can get quiet and pray. I can believe Sunday is coming, if not as quickly as I'd like. I can remember that lonely Saturdays can be good for a girl, in a stretching kind of way, if I can accept them and not divert the grief into manic activity or bags of cheese puffs, if I can think back to other Saturdays (and there've been plenty) that eventually gave way to something wobbly and new.

What does your Saturday look like? Are you waiting on a job? On a check? Is your kid sick? Do you need to forgive...or be forgiven? Are you doubled up with resentment, or worn down with longing? Whatever it is, remember your other Saturdays. Know that others have traveled this path. Trust, even if it seems a longshot. Call someone who's pro-You. Pray. Chocolate never hurts.

Sunday will come.

How do you wait through discomfort, loss, or fear?

Who are your Saturday friends?

ONE VERSE FOR THOUGHT:
When you go through deep waters, I will be with you. When you go through rivers of difficulty, you will not drown. When you walk through the fire of oppression, you will not be burned up; the flames will not consume you. **–Isaiah 43:2, NLT**

9

one more chance

ON GETTING REAL, FAILING WELL, AND TASTING REDEMPTION

the gifts of pain

One of my favorite single moms recently celebrated her fifth year of sobriety. If you heard her story, you'd feel like a total weenie for complaining about anything ever, but she is remarkably grateful and optimistic, and also realistic that if she doesn't keep walking the walk, her four-year-old son will be lost to her. And she's too in love with and dedicated to him to let that happen.

I used to think I was the one schlepping the boxes back on the loading dock when the **How To Do Life** manuals were distributed. For so many years, it looked like everyone else was happy and knew what to do and how to be, and I was just faking it the best I could…but still not good enough. Now I realize that looks are deceiving and we all have our choice of painkillers when life is just too much. Some are more socially acceptable (working 80 hours per week or overexercising); others—overeating, smoking, drinking and drugging—not so much. But the place deep in us that screams for relief is very real, and the more we acknowledge, address, and attend to it—without anesthetizing it—the better off we'll be.

Of course this is far harder and more painful than we would hope. Perhaps one of the scariest but most beneficial occurrences in the years since my divorce was realizing it wasn't all his fault. This reality hit me harder than I'd have expected, because it opened up the floodgates to all the hurts and the subsequent damaging ways I learned to deal with life. I remember thinking I might possibly die if the secrets I carried saw the light of day, and the coming-back process (assuming I survived) was going to be brutal. But then, I looked at my daughter and thought: *I do not want her to repeat my life.* Terrified but determined, I descended into the pit, the anesthesia wore off, and I cried and railed and despaired. I ended some addictions and then uncovered others. I wrestle still, but I'm getting better.

If you are drinking too much, working too much, eating too much, purging too much, spending too much, *feeling* too much, there is a way back that will heal both you and your kids. You are strong enough to emerge from the pit. Really. Find a 12-Step group and/or someone you trust and love, and give words and voice to the things you swore you'd never say. There's freedom on the other side.

How do you deal with the pain of living, longing, and hoping?

What is your "drug" of choice?

ONE VERSE FOR THOUGHT:

For we do not have a high priest who is unable to empathize with our weaknesses, but we have one who has been tempted in every way, just as we are—yet he did not sin. Let us then approach God's throne of grace with confidence, so that we may receive mercy and find grace to help us in our time of need. **–Hebrews 4:15-16, NIV**

lost and found

When I was married, I desperately tried to make my life look good. It was a total sham, but I wanted to seem like I had a happy, orderly life so as to keep happy, orderly people around me. I kept it light and breezy around most everyone, fearing that going any deeper would reveal secrets I wasn't ready to tell and jinx my chance at happy. Shallow though they were, those relationships kept me going; I liked to tell myself I still fell within the range of "normal" because I was still married.

But when we become newly single, we may find one of the harder things to handle is being cut off *completely*. Formerly cohesive families can split and take sides; friends can drift away, fearing divorce is contagious; churches may blame and shame us for not keeping our partners happy. In the end, we can stand alone.

Grieving the loss, aching for our kids, feeling lonely out of our minds…these are not qualities that draw The Happy Ones close. There can be redemption in the ache, though. In teaching the Parable of the Lost Son in the Book of Luke, Pastor John Ortberg described something called *Kezazah*, which was a cutting-off ceremony reserved for those who tried to return to community after something seemingly unforgiveable happens. In the parable, the wandering son squandered his inheritance and shamed the father; if he tried to return, the townspeople were prepared to cast him out, breaking a clay pot at his feet to symbolize the relationship was irretrievably broken. But God is all about relationship, especially after crisis. Instead we find the father scanning the horizon, waiting, having already forgiven. When the lost son finally returns, broken and humbled, the father runs to greet him, welcoming him back in the fold before anyone can stop him. The son is no longer outcast, but part-of.

What if we *rushed* to greet the lonely, the scared, the lost and broken in our midst? What if being without community in our darkest hours was simply not a possibility? When we're willing to give up the illusion that all is well, we're finally ready to get real. We may ache for a smoother path but there is richness in the struggle, *which is made for sharing*, as we find our way back home.

In what ways did you feel cut off after your separation or divorce?

How could a community of those who struggle help you and your children heal?

One Verse for Thought:

…But while he was still a long way off, his father saw him and was filled with compassion for him; he ran to his son, threw his arms around him and kissed him. The son said to him, "Father, I have sinned against heaven and against you. I am no longer worthy to be called your son." But the father said to his servants, "Quick! Bring the best robe and put it on him. Put a ring on his finger and sandals on his feet. Bring the fattened calf and kill it. Let's have a feast and celebrate. For this son of mine was dead and is alive again; he was lost and is found." So they began to celebrate. **–Luke 15:20-24, NIV**

pick your poison

When I talk with single moms whose exes act like stereotypical Disney Dads who buy plenty of toys but have skipped out on child support, I tell them one of my favorite prayers following my divorce was, "God? Please come down and hammer his ass. Amen."

Sometimes holding a grudge can become the reason we get up every morning, but then the anger and bitterness will start to get the best of us—of all we are and all we will be. Our righteous indignation can keep us stuck in the mire, and then we start to hate *that* even more.

I remember sensing God saying at the time, *You need to let this go, because it will all come to its logical end.* Frankly, I didn't want to wait that long; this was already year six of our glacially slow county justice system's cat-and-mouse game with my former husband's back child support. But what I really didn't want to let go of was my need for vindication and justice. I wanted to wear the white hat, to win, to be on the moral high ground and slightly martyred. What's wrong with that?

I didn't realize it costs just as much to stay a victim as it does to *not* be one…maybe even more. To move on costs some pride and some sense of fairness in the world. It costs some faith, because if God isn't in the vindication business then what's the point? And later, down the road, it costs some forgiveness for the one who hurt you, which may be completely undeserved but is absolutely necessary. But to *not* move on? That costs us a whole life of mistrust and resentment that erodes everything from the inside.

I think the only way out of being a victim is trusting and remembering God will turn things for good. Note this may or may not entail the ass-hammering we are hoping for but, by acknowledging God is there and can help us through and out of victimhood (even when it's justified), we can move toward healing.

After years of this particular fight, I had to turn my trust to God and ask Him to meet our needs. I did not do this very willingly or gracefully, but He has provided, in big ways and small, and mostly freed me from that prison of resentment. When I start getting on my high horse of injustice, I have to stop and remember. Sometimes it takes us learning the hard way that we can't have it both ways: victim *and* victor. Ask Him to help you choose the better.

In which areas of your life do you feel marginalized or victimized?

What would it look like to give up any hope of having those wrongs righted?

ONE VERSE FOR THOUGHT:

No one can serve two masters. Either you will hate the one and love the other, or you will be devoted to the one and despise the other... –**Matthew 6:24, NIV**

one generation removed

Our worship leader, Jay, spoke one Father's Day about what the holiday means to people. Some, he acknowledged, feel a tremendous tenderness for their dads on this day; others feel pain. As he discussed his own father, Jay explained that, because of him, he was one generation removed from potential harm. It was his father who made the move away from brokenness and pain and toward God. Without that choice, Jay relayed, he would be in a completely different place.

I thought of my brother and I, and how we were raised, and how we made some big mistakes. For myself, I had neither the inkling, wherewithal, nor stamina to connect all the dots before I picked a husband; I was simply afraid no one else would ask. I had no blueprint for a good marriage, nor any examples around me. Late in the game, in the midst of excruciating divorces, my brother and I made the decision for God—to help us, to help our kids. You'd think it would have been some sweetly ethereal moment of conversion, but there were and are repercussions, and a rending that occurs when we finally see some truth.

For years, I wanted God to absolve me of my bad choices; instead He has redeemed them. Through a lot of pain, I have become a parent who can teach her daughter how to live in the midst of incongruity and ambivalence, because He is teaching me how. So many of the single moms I meet in Eve's Daughters grew up in hard, hard circumstances and yet are lightyears ahead of their own parents. What choice did they make? Only that they would do better—somehow, some way—for their kids.

The irony of course is that "better" oftentimes looks like "alone"; many of us have had to literally distance ourselves from people practicing addiction, abuse, and adultery to provide a stable, honest household for our kids. We've had to let go—of people and plans—and forge a new path. And despite how society might judge, I believe God honors these excruciating choices when we turn to Him, keeping His promises to us, to our kids.

What I've learned over the years is that He wastes nothing, and generations can be redeemed by the slow and steady choice to do the next right thing. Just imagine where your kids will be if you keep walking this road with Him…another generation removed from harm, moving toward healing.

How have you created a new path for your kids since you've been a single mom?

In what ways is your parenting better or worse from how you were parented?

ONE VERSE FOR THOUGHT:
If it is disagreeable in your sight to serve the Lord, choose for yourselves today whom you will serve: whether the gods which your fathers served which were beyond the River, or the gods of the Amorites in whose land you are living; but as for me and my house, we will serve the Lord.
–Joshua 24:15, NASB

getting into alignment

When I was walking my dog recently, an older woman came up to me and said, "I had a golden retriever, too. Smartest dog I ever met. Flunked out of obedience training multiple times and continually escaped from the back yard, but he knew to look both ways before crossing the street as he ran away."

The incongruity of her statements made me laugh, but it's far less funny when we ourselves live that way. In her excellent book, **My Grandfather's Blessings**, author and physician Rachel Naomi Remen shared an experiment in which she asked 73 physicians to rank-order the same list twice with 21 life values (things like control, admiration, love, power, success, kindness, etc.), first with regard to their work lives and second with regard to their personal lives. Shockingly, none made two identical lists, meaning the way they lived professionally was not in alignment with the way they lived personally, and many were dismayed to learn they believed one way while living another. In the end, she believes we *all* tend to sacrifice integrity to expediency, and it damages how we live.

When I think of my own life, I'd rank *competency* and *professionalism* as highly desirable on my work list...but *tenderness* and *transparency*, which I'd want in my daily life, might get me fired. I also might believe I want to be successful as a parent, but if I don't act consistently with regard to discipline, or if I routinely make promises I don't keep, then success is only something I want but am not willing to work for: I'd believe one way and live another.

As you well know, it can be exhausting being one person at work, one person at home, one person with our parents and siblings and another with our friends; living incongruently takes a toll. I don't know what it would look like to live as though I have two identical lists—to be authentic across the board: from worker bee to mom to woman to friend to Christian. But maybe it's worth writing our own lists and seeing where we diverge, so we can come back to center. By doing so we demonstrate to our children that they, too, can learn to live truly as integrated, as one, as possible.

In which areas of your life are you most out of alignment with your beliefs and values?

How can you start living in a way that's more congruent with the person you want to be?

ONE VERSE FOR THOUGHT:
For I do not do the good I want to do, but the evil I do not want to do—this I keep on doing… **–Romans 7:19, NIV**

putting the pieces together

My Eve's Daughters business partner, Cathy, loves doing puzzles; I am spatially stunted. She focuses on the destination; I only see the next mile marker. She is comfortable with the 30,000-foot view; I'm scrambling for a detailed road map.

How in the world did we hatch a nonprofit?

I find it interesting we were put together for this venture in that our strengths, weaknesses, and hearts were in such different locales. It's been confusing, messy, liberating, exciting, and exhausting all at once, kind of like single parenting. The fits and starts were almost always unexplainable until we got to the other side of them, until the full picture started coming into view.

I landed in a place I never wanted to be, doing what I never wanted to do, and finding my heart broken for others in similar situations. I could not have visualized this for myself.

Of course I planned on happily-ever-after. Of course the choice to divorce created fallout, both positive and negative, that I couldn't have foreseen. But just as with a puzzle, when you finally get some pieces to fit and say, "Oh! It's an *apple*, not a fire plug," your vision can shift toward something that didn't exist before, making it more real than you knew.

I've been a single parent for the vast majority of my daughter's life. We've slogged through illnesses, work challenges, parenting conundrums, money shortages, health scares, legal battles, loneliness, and regular, boring life stuff. At every turn, I realize now, I've received another piece of the puzzle. Some hard-won lessons are the equivalent of a corner piece—an anchor securely gained. Others are blurry insiders—parts that make no sense at the moment, parts that need to be put aside for a bit before they fit.

Both are needed. Both are valid. But I believe more and more that ours is a God who hides the box top. And, paradoxically, that can benefit us by honing our vision and stretching our sights beyond what we ourselves can imagine.

Which challenges in your life make more sense to you now that some time and miles have elapsed?

How do you keep focused on the big picture, so you don't drown in the details?

ONE VERSE FOR THOUGHT:
And we know that God causes everything to work together for the good of those who love God and are called according to his purpose for them. **–Romans 8:28, NLT**

feeling it

The Myers-Briggs personality test defines me as an INFJ, one of the roughly three percent of the population who are otherwise known as freakishly and hopelessly hyper-sensitive. There are actual support groups for people like us who find it excruciating to be in the world most days. I have fought my oversensitivity my whole life, to no avail. And while it's true if I could toughen up certain comments wouldn't hurt so badly, it's also true I've tolerated some really blaming, terrible behavior from others who have gutted me and then said it's my fault for feeling badly.

Recently, when asking someone gently and collaboratively for some behavior changes, I got blamed for many extraneous things…but no accountability for the original offense. Blogger and author Glennon Doyle Melton suggests if we can respond to feelings with curiosity instead of fear, we can get invited deeper into the relationship. So, if someone says, "You really hurt me," and we respond with, "I'm so sorry. Tell me what you're feeling," we're welcoming the opportunity to go deeper.

Sadly, sometimes we invite others into our hearts, into an area they haven't known, and it's received as warmly as an invitation to Siberia in January. In other words, *No, thanks*. But as I thought about Melton's words, I also wondered… how many times over the years have I caught myself suggesting *my daughter* "shouldn't" feel something? How many times have I told *myself* that? It's so easy as single parents to get caught up in our heads, trying to keep everyone rowing in the same direction, that we don't have the time, energy, or inclination to deal with hurt feelings or misunderstandings.

It's so much easier to tell ourselves *Don't even go there.* But if we don't, those feelings still remain, festering and inflaming, until a smallish offense becomes a relational deal-breaker.

What if our response was, first, *I'm sorry*, and second, *Help me understand*? Instead of telling our kids, "Don't be upset; I'm sure your friend didn't mean it that way," we can say, "I'm so sorry. Tell me more." The decision to engage clears away the debris so we don't make a wreckage of our relationships. And best of all, we always get to issue that invitation.

How do you react when someone hurts your feelings?

In which ways can you invite deeper conversation with your kids? Your friends? Your colleagues?

ONE VERSE FOR THOUGHT:
Everyone may think his own way of living is right, but the Eternal examines our hearts. **–Proverbs 21:2, VOICE**

worst foot forward

After getting an assignment years ago to write two gift books on parenting, I foolishly got uber-holy and asked God which topics to tackle. Immediately I got the vision of perhaps my worst mothering moment to date. And then I got a lot less holy and started begging: "Oh, please, no…not *that*." When I got the book outline and learned that particular topic would be the first chapter in the single mom book, I asked again: "*Really*? You want me to lead with the screaming mom story?"

I wrestled with this because I care deeply about how I appear. Not so much my hair and hips, but whether I seem competent, polished, knowledgeable. If I kicked off this book with this particular episode, how was I going to *look* here? And He said, as He does often, *Please just shut up and write*, because doing a good job in His eyes can mean simple obedience and a willingness to look foolish or fail. This of course contrasts dramatically with doing a good job in the world's eyes, which looks more like polished, air-brushed perfection.

Single moms, especially, seem to have more to worry about as the judgments can fly fast and furious in our direction when our kids are less than angelic. Years ago, my daughter was having a pouty fit in her room and actually *opened her window so she could sob pitifully out of it.* And all I could think was, "Oy, the neighbors, wondering about that poor, poor child and that hateful single mom…" It takes faith to be willing to lose face publicly when trying to be consistent with discipline, transparency and connection in our relationships. But would you want a life without those things?

Regarding those books, I led with the worst—we all did, the four moms who wrote the series—and was humbled and tickled to find that people were reading and laughing and recognizing themselves in our collective writings. It's like they had permission finally to say, *"Yeah, baby*—I've been there, too. Did I ever tell you about the time…?" And we're all off and running.

Part of my dream for community—especially a community built on faith—is a willingness to look bad on the surface because people know the grace they'll receive is so much deeper. In some areas, we've got so many miles to go…but what a remarkably freeing thing it is to live and parent and support and shine without all that "look-good" getting in the way.

What are you most concerned about, appearances-wise?

How do you keep your fears of being less-than-perfect out of your kids' lives?

ONE VERSE FOR THOUGHT:
For by grace you have been saved through faith. And this is not your own doing; it is the gift of God, not a result of works, so that no one may boast. **–Ephesians 2:8-9, ESV**

redemption

As part of an exercise recently, I had to write down an overview of my life story. Let me just say it was interesting. In some ways I feel a million miles away from the person I was writing about, like I barely recognized her anymore, and yet (of course), everything was deeply personal and familiar. Surprisingly, what I noticed most was the redemption that's occurred; thank God (literally) I was not left behind in those years.

But I also remember vividly, with a startling amount of tenderness, that girl who was so perfectionistic she would not allow a mistake on her watch; who was shamed silent over parts of her past; who worked hard, head down, trying to stay under the radar for decades. All she wanted to do was hide. It would take many years and miles to believe that others needed to hear—and could benefit from hearing—her story.

I have longed to build community and break the isolation that's so common in single parenting; we all ache for friendship and family, sharing a meal and doing life together. There is beauty in single parents taking a deep breath and taking it a step further, willing to be transparent with others about their lives—their sometimes messy, unpredictable, unflattering lives. They know what the secrets and lost years could cost them—and their children—and that cost is too high.

Here's the amazing thing: The ones who thought there would be no redemption for them—the ones for whom abuse, addiction, or neglect were normal—shine like the sun as they arrange the beautiful, jagged pieces of their lives on display. And you know what? That gives others permission to share both the lovely and unlovely parts of their lives as well. And what a breathtaking thing it is to witness.

One of my pastors told me gently many years ago that God would break my heart for the best of reasons and then ask me to give the pieces away. As a relative newbie to the faith, I wondered whether that meant He was a sadist. Now, I see the great wisdom: My brokenness allows your brokenness, and your brokenness allows others'. We're connected through our weaknesses, not our strengths, and by sharing these freely, we give permission to those journeying with us to come out of hiding and live in the light.

As you gain strength and ability in your parenting, which parts of your life are being redeemed?

What part of your story could you share with another single parent toward greater transparency and healing?

ONE VERSE FOR THOUGHT:
Whoever is a believer in Christ is a new creation. The old way of living has disappeared. A new way of living has come into existence. **–2 Corinthians 5:17, GW**

for a little while

Poring over my daughter's senior photos, I remember. It was autumn of 2001 when we left our family home and moved into our townhouse, which had been owned forever by a lovely elderly couple. No work had been done on the place since approximately 1970, and I look back and wonder what I was thinking, because I said, OK, sure! I'll take the floral Brady Bunch wallpaper, the worn avocado shag, and the fringed orange curtains, and I'll renovate this place and turn it into a home for us, but just for a little while because bigger things are on the horizon.

I remember looking into the school district before I purchased, smiling to myself because elementary school was still several years off; I surely did not need to know about the middle or high schools because we'd be gone by then. But I bought the unit and started anyway, reeling from a gutting divorce with a newly contrary three-year-old and a cancer-riddled, 95-pound lab mix, feathering our nest until we could fly somewhere better.

Six weeks in the dog's cancer got too big to fix, and so on a dark December night, I laid on the floor in the office of a vet I'd just met in my new neighborhood, sobbing harder than I had in my whole life while holding that sick dog as he passed and carried with him so much of my grief over the end of my marriage, and the questions, and the fury. I cried long after I left the vet that night, screaming alone in the car and telling God He really needed to step it up because I simply could not take another loss.

So then it was just me and Em. I worked and I raised her as best I could and I nested. She moved from Kindercare into first grade, and days turned into years. The grief lessened and I learned how to soften, and she grew taller and learned how to toughen, and survived the middle school I never investigated because we were to be gone by then. And it was always her and I, in our temporary home, because I was keeping my eyes on the horizon.

We are here, 15 years hence. I am nesting still. BeBe the Gassy Wonder Dog has joined us after years without a pet— the years that were tough and lean, when budgeting for a doctor's bill was far more important than a vet bill—and has added a sweetness to the mix. I call her my furry daughter, and I got her to help ease the transition that is coming, the one that starts with those photos.

I look at who Em's becoming and see the shy girl in flouncy-butt leggings and the shivering girl in a Blues Clues swimsuit and the sad girl who feels different from the others and the stubborn girl who is going to try something hard and the sweet girl who loves and forgives, and they are all there in those deep blue eyes…every age, every stage. And here in our temporary home, every tree that was decorated and egg that was hunted and bath that was read through and meals that were savored and lessons that were taught and learned are held in these walls.

I'm learning Em has always called this home, not temporary…but only for maybe one more year, because she is keeping her eyes on the horizon.

How have you provided stability for your kids?

In what ways do you think life "elsewhere" would be better or easier?

ONE VERSE FOR THOUGHT:
So teach us to number our days that we may get a heart of wisdom. **–Psalm 90:12, ESV**

10

one moment of hope

ON FINDING JOY,
KNOWING PEACE, AND
LOOKING FORWARD

great expectations

My friend Cindy bought me a bracelet years ago with a single silver heart engraved with the word *hope*. It is especially meaningful because, at the time, she didn't have much money and I didn't have much hope. But like good friends do, she chose to invest and encourage me. Between the bracelet getting older and getting banged around, it's developed its own beautiful patina—just like we do—and is a dangling definition of what can happen when we keep hope close at hand.

Writer Os Hillman suggests the most difficult place to keep moving in faith is when we're in extreme pain, especially emotional pain. This is where our hope can take a beating, where we can become paralyzed, desperate, and dejected. Proverbs 13:12 states that hope deferred makes the heart sick, but Psalm 126:5 says that those who sow in tears will reap with songs of joy. This is easier said than done; sowing in the midst of tears takes diligence and dedication and the ability to envision a different future. Hillman wisely notes we can't do this if we're relying on our feelings alone; those will tell us we shouldn't bother because everything's hopeless. It's only the perseverance of slogging through that brings us to a beautiful harvest.

What farmer would scatter seed without the hope of the bounty? What would be the point? I see so many single moms pouring themselves out for their kids in the midst of the most uncertain circumstances, and it's the hope that keeps them fluid—hope for today, hope for tomorrow, hope for the person their little one will become.

They can't see the future, but they sow anyway.

Hope keeps us going when everything around us is changing. I have friends and family in myriad storms of life, love, and health, big life changes and small, and yet the ones who best weather the winds are the ones who still reach out to provide shelter for others, protecting and encouraging them now with the anticipation of a brighter future.

How have you learned to sow in the midst of tears?

What kind of harvest do you envision for your children?

ONE VERSE FOR THOUGHT:
We must continue to hold firmly to our declaration of faith. The one who made the promise is faithful.
–Hebrews 10:23, GW

scatter joy

It's surprising sometimes, the ways in which life works itself out. In our house, we're navigating teenhood and all that comes with it. Some days are better than others but, honestly, I feel pretty solid that we'll make it through and that whatever we don't know or have now will show up if and when we need it. I'm also keenly aware that I have a tribe surrounding me, including family, friends, colleagues and, when necessary, paid professionals. Somehow, the whole clan of us, we're managing.

Joy is a funny thing. We can confuse it with happiness, but the latter is more transient, capricious: You can't count on it sticking around. Joy, on the other hand, is anchored deep; it's like a knowing contentment, set in concrete. It may not reflect your circumstances, but perhaps something more valuable—that everything will come out in the wash, more or less. I'm well aware that my tribe and I have some joy going on, and it's not a state of mind I want to take for granted. The only reason we can welcome joy is because we survived its opposite, sorrow—just as much as we celebrate the light after stumbling in the darkness.

Sometimes life as a single mom can feel like a triathlon, times ten, and it's easy to forget 1) we actually can have joy and 2) we can share it freely in the midst of the mundane. Think about the millions of things you do, and wish for, and encourage in your kids. Or for your friends. Or at your job. Or in the community. The essence of your joy comes from a place of knowing (yes, sometimes sorrowful knowing), yet transforms into something remarkable in the giving.

A friend sent me a little reminder in the mail: that I am enough, that she sees what I cannot, and that I need to take care of my heart so I can keep scattering joy. Sometimes, just one person caring is the fuel to keep us going.

Who can you remind today that he or she is no longer alone, with lots to give? Scatter on.

When was the last time you felt joy?

Which areas of your life are most joyous right now…even in their imperfections?

ONE VERSE FOR THOUGHT:
…and those the Lord has rescued will return. They will enter Zion with singing; everlasting joy will crown their heads. Gladness and joy will overtake them, and sorrow and sighing will flee away. **–Isaiah 35:10, NIV**

all things new

September has become my favorite time of year because, to me, it signifies a clean slate, a grand re-do. Close your eyes: Remember the sawdusty smell of freshly sharpened No. 2 pencils? A new tip meant a new start: new class, new friends, mulligans for all, with hope abounding.

When my daughter comes home from her first day of the new school year and tells me it was awesome, my heart always leaps, relieved, as I've wondered about her all day and whether her fresh start was a good one. She always teases me on those mornings, asking if I am going to cry like I did when she started first grade.

I tell her it's kinda like first grade again, except she's taller. This September will mark her last first day, and I will beg to take a picture of her holding her lunchbox like she did in first grade, back when she was all Scooby Doo and one front tooth.

Fresh backpack, fresh start. My heart aches, grateful.

I cannot tell you how or why, but it feels like I'm getting a do-over as well. I have been quietly thankful, not entirely sure of the circumstances or how long they'll last. But I feel supported, buoyed by a clear course. I'm no longer rudderless as I was in the early days of my divorce. It feels to me like an early Thanksgiving—purposeful but humble, jubilant but shy. It took a long time, but I'm becoming new.

I talked to an old friend recently who's known me since I was 12. I told her about this strange state I'm in; she told me I was due, and I smiled. The newness is tempered by the full knowing that life continues to twist and turn, to present challenges and those ubiquitous "growth opportunities" that "build character." As if we need any more of that. Things will break; homework will perplex; doctors' bills will come. Nothing really changes, but everything does, seemingly. Something has shifted, and I think it has to do with purpose, direction, understanding, and maybe some hard-won wisdom.

Enjoy the strange newness of September as well, and see whether what seems like an ending is more of a beginning.

What would a fresh start look like for you?

How do you talk to your kids about change being life's only constant?

ONE VERSE FOR THOUGHT:
Then King David went in and sat before the Lord and said, "Who am I, O Lord God, and what is my house, that you have brought me thus far? And this was a small thing in your eyes, O God. You have also spoken of your servant's house for a great while to come, and have shown me future generations... **–1 Chronicles, 17:16-17, ESV**

peace out

When I was divorcing and struggling with the ever-present rancor, my dear friend, Kathy, sent me a prayer that ended "...and peace will be written on your doorpost." Today, I have plaques over my front and back doors marked with the word *peace*. It's not about peace at any price (by squelching feelings and ignoring problems) but rather an overarching commitment to talking, listening, loving, and disagreeing well.

It cost me a lot of peace to get to today, but some days I still forget. I remember once being so angry with my daughter that I said, "Just go to your room. I can't even talk to you right now." As she walked dejectedly toward the stairs, I asked, "WHAT WERE YOU THINKING?" She turned to answer my question, but, waving my hand, I snapped, "Just go upstairs. I don't want to talk about it anymore tonight."

Two seconds later, I blurted out: "Did you *really* think that was going to work for you?" She froze, one foot on a stair, one on the landing, waiting for me to make up my mind, while I wondered when, precisely, I had lost it. On that day, I forgot about peace...and we both paid the price for it. What could have been a mature, respectful conversation devolved into an angry, crazy, half-silence of my own doing.

My friend Blyma explained to me the Jewish people have a phrase, *shalom bayit*, meaning "peace in the house." The expression holds the expectation that one will watch one's words and actions and weigh them against whether they'll add or subtract peace from the household. Do it well, and experience a type of joy that comes from being in your family groove. Do it poorly, and experience how toxic that silent anger can be, magnifying the space between family members.

We as single parents don't always have a handy counter-balance to our frustration, disappointment, or anger, but it is up to us to create, maintain, and value *shalom bayit* anyway. Study after study has suggested that stable households (yes, those include single parent households as well) produce stable kids. And isn't that our greatest desire?

How do you keep the peace in your household?

What would shalom bayit *look like for your family on a daily basis?*

ONE VERSE FOR THOUGHT:

Don't let even one rotten word seep out of your mouths. Instead, offer only fresh words that build others up when they need it most. That way your good words will communicate grace to those who hear them. **–Ephesians 4:29, VOICE**

and one more thing...

Have you ever been in a season where you're running on fumes for various reasons? For me right now, work is kinda crazy, parenting is kinda crazy, and my personal odometer passed 50, which is utterly crazy. I confess I'm not handling it very gracefully as I wrestle with the life I have versus the life I envisioned. And just as I was trying to balance all of this, one more thing happened that will require much patience, perseverance, and, frankly, more than I feel I have to give at this point.

Of course you know what I'm talking about—how hard it is to find hope when one more thing hits. I meet with our moms and hear how school loans are delayed, jobs are insecure, and kids are struggling. I listen to frightened responses about late child support checks (or the prospect of no child support check ever), the possibility of running out of food, or the notices to disconnect utilities. There can be great hopelessness and wondering whether things will ever get any easier.

Pastor Rick Warren has written extensively about grace and hope, and perhaps the greatest takeaway was his reminder that the Bible holds literally thousands of promises waiting to be claimed. Now, I excel at worrying, conniving and plotting during life crises, but so often I forget to claim these promises for my little family. One of my favorites, Jeremiah 29:11 ("For I know the plans I have for you," says the Lord. "They are plans for good and not for disaster, to give you a future and a hope"), was written in the midst of life-gone-wrong, not happily-ever-after. We need to remember it was meant not as an escape, but an encouragement when one more thing threatened to derail our last bit of hope.

Within your single mom community, you will find a support system of amazing women who will help you stand up when you can't do it on your own. As we wobble forward in life, I wish for you and your kids that hope will meet you daily, and that you have the strength to face one more thing... together.

What do you do when one more thing threatens to upset your balance?

How do you help your children cope when life starts to feel overwhelming?

ONE VERSE FOR THOUGHT:
Be still before the Lord and wait patiently for him...
–Psalm 37:7, ESV

realistic hope

At Eve's Daughters, we love the phrase "realistic hope." Cathy and I loved it so much that it was part of our original mission statement—the idea that we couldn't promise Mr. Fabulous would show up and take care of all your problems, but we could promise support and community while you took care of your family. When I first divorced, I sure wished someone would have waved a magic wand and fixed everything. But as time went by and I continued to experience challenges, I felt like a kid playing a Whack-a-Mole game: One problem would go down, but two more would pop up.

I recently had an opportunity to just sit and listen to a single mom. We were thrown together inadvertently and had since become friends. The greater gift, though, came earlier that morning, while it was still so dark it felt like it would never be light again. I'd prayed to be encouraging to her when we met and I heard a Scripture reference, which I wrote on a purple Post-It® and stuck in my purse. Later when we met, I pulled it out and asked, "Does this mean anything to you?" Well. Of course it did. It was timely and precious and pertinent in a way I could not manufacture. I gave her a hug and told her to place it on her bathroom mirror. She laughed and said she was going to stick it to her forehead and have everyone read it back to her.

On that same day, I had a great crisis with someone I love, because something was done that cannot be undone. And with the day not even close to done, it did kinda feel like I was up to my knees. That day the heartache mole raised its pointy little head, but the childrearing and financial drama moles were still snug in their holes. For now. But for some reason I didn't feel as yanked around as I usually do. I felt human, to be sure, but not the need to be superhuman. I felt brokenhearted, but thankful. Tired, but energized. Alone, but not so.

And I believe that—wading through, eyes on the horizon, tiredly rejoicing—is realistic hope.

What helps you keep your eyes on the future?

What does "realistic hope" look like to you, and how can you help your children and yourself to better deal with the messiness of life?

ONE VERSE FOR THOUGHT:

Not only so, but we also glory in our sufferings, because we know that suffering produces perseverance; perseverance, character; and character, hope. And hope does not put us to shame, because God's love has been poured out into our hearts through the Holy Spirit, who has been given to us.
–Romans 5:3-5, NIV

grace and peace

There are people in my life who sign all their emails with "Cheers!" or "Blessings" or "Best." But one in particular uses "Grace and Peace." This simple phrase weaves in and out of Paul's letters in the New Testament, almost always followed by "...to you from God the Father and the Lord Jesus Christ." It's something I've read dozens of times that's never sunk in until recently.

Another Thanksgiving, and, yeah, I'm supposed to be thankful. But sometimes it can feel like an impossible assignment. There are always loved ones struggling in some capacity, unmet needs, unfulfilled hopes. There's that stupid extra weight, or health challenges, or a shortage of time, or a conflict or three.

Things are not always as I would have them.

The grace part—the thing that smooths out the edges and makes each new day at least marginally doable—has to come first. And since that's an undeserved gift we can't manufacture for ourselves, we've got to keep aware of its existence. We've all been shown it, likely at some of our worst moments; it's the grease that keeps things running.

And then peace—glorious peace—follows. Likely you've had a glimpse of this, too: the baby finally falls asleep, the job finally comes through, the check finally arrives, the teen finally gets home (even if it's 3 a.m.). It can range from a fleeting moment to sheer relief to some stunningly clear vision, in the midst of imperfection.

You know peace when you feel it, just as you know what life feels like in its absence.

Somehow on that Thanksgiving morning, in between making a disgusting turkey hand puppet to completely gross out my daughter (because I love to make her laugh), to talking to my big brother, to anticipating a houseful of friends because we don't have much family nearby, I accepted some grace and got the peace to boot. I was so incredibly aware of their presence I hardly knew what to do with myself.

I don't have any illusions that this will last. And that's OK—grace and peace will come again. But for now, I feel them, this remarkable duo, on either side of me as I type, and I'm more thankful than I've been in a long time.

What does grace look like in your life?

How do you and your children claim peace in the midst of life's uncertainties?

ONE VERSE FOR THOUGHT:
May God give you more and more grace and peace as you grow in your knowledge of God and Jesus our Lord.
–2 Peter 1:2, NLT

ancient beauty

Do you remember your first "ma'am"? As I recall, I was appalled and highly offended, addressed by something like a 12-year-old while I was still a relative youngster in my twenties.

These days, I'm lucky I'm not called worse. When I got a surprise discount recently at Ross Dress for Less, I thought I was special; instead, the cashier told me it was Senior Tuesday. Sadly, I am not a senior. I might have been in my workout pants, with little makeup, but still: *Way to gut a girl, Ross.*

I never was one of those women who got to rely on my looks very much, but things definitely were more promising several decades ago. I've also battled my whole life with depression, addiction, and body issues and maybe, like me, you're finding things are not getting any easier, firmer, or healthier with age. But something better is happening to us that's worthy of excitement: We're becoming *beautiful.* We may be *ma'am*ed more than we'd like, and we may not be able to sleep through the night anymore, but the years are making us so much more calm than we used to be. Maybe it's the wearing effect of the children, that our synapses are shot, but I like to think it's because we've survived so much that some of the excess worry has just left the scene. There's a peace that comes from that, and beauty is one of the byproducts.

My neighbor is an 81-year-old single mom who survived The Great Depression, multiple wars, ovarian cancer that should have killed her in her twenties, and far more. She hurts every day and has for years; she's had so many surgeries in the time I've known her I tease her she's being replaced, part by part, to become SuperMarge. A couple weeks ago, she announced proudly that she'd joined the drum corps over at the local senior center.

Of course she did.

She also warned me it would be getting pretty loud Monday afternoons at 3:30 when the corps came over to practice at her place…like she was warning me she was hosting a kegger. The whole thought of it made me smile.

She is one of the more beautiful women I know, simply because she's survived so very much.

The same is true for us, having endured the unsettledness of solo parenting. There is a knowing that surfaces, not arrogant and blowsy, but silent and strong, when we've tackled the ER and an empty bank account and multiple trips to court and special needs constraints and still *know* we can make it through. It shines in our eyes and shows in our hard-won wrinkles. What we single moms trade in beauty sleep, flat stomachs, and Nordstrom half yearly sales we more than make up for in the splendor of our strength. It is hope, on display.

Has anyone told you lately how beautiful you are?

When you think of all you've survived in your life, what words would you use to describe yourself?

How do you stay away from comparing yourself to others?

ONE VERSE FOR THOUGHT:
He has made everything beautiful in its time.
–Ecclesiastes 3:11, NIV

joy in the morning

I was sitting at my dining room table one morning, looking at the decorative blocks that spell JOY on the side table, and I started to cry and to smile. Somehow it hit me—where Em and I are at, how many miles this journey has been, how close to one significant finish line we are. How deeply grateful I am, for all the years I begged God for wisdom and clearer direction and a guarantee of safety and provision when I was poor and afraid, and look what He did and where we landed.

My girl is still sleeping, beat from her initiation as one of the newest Color Guard members. We've been living rehearsals three times per week, plus ten 12-hour days of band camp. It gets worse when school starts. Blisters, aches, hydrating—we are not athletes, so we are learning as we go. When I picked her up last night, she was exhausted, sweaty, wind-burned. Also, confident, belonging, laughing. She said in the car recently, "I'm just...really happy." What more could I ask?

For a woman who always wanted more kids, I'm finding myself happy to sign up to host an o-dark-thirty, pre-competition breakfast for eight rental daughters, making French toast and French braids, fueling them for a 15-hour day that will last in their memories.

And so the tears that morning flowed from the realization of what came up to this point—all the midnight fevers and brokenness and worry of whether we'd have enough (and whether I was enough) and for all the things I braced myself against that never came to pass but helped contribute to my growing gray hair population. This has been the ride of

my life, and very soon, this part of it—this day-to-day, con-
versational, silly, snapping, eye-rolling, loving, deep-talking,
practical joking, messy, life-planning chapter—will close and
open to…what? As a single mom for almost 15 years, what's
next? I'm so excited to see what God has in store for her; who
He made her to be is just coming into focus.

But oh, the changes this will entail.

Through my tears, those blocks that have over the years
called to me, reminded me, mocked me, challenged me, that
day they made sense. I thought, even in the midst of the unknown, this is joy, spilling out. How amazing is that?

Where do you search for joy?

How do you savor it when it shines and remember it when it hides?

ONE VERSE FOR THOUGHT:
…Weeping may last through the night, but joy comes with
the morning. **–Psalm 30:5, NLT**

the end of this journey

As Em drove us to the coast yesterday, I explained my directions, telling her we'd go past an indoor playground she attended many years prior. "I remember having a great time there!" she said, while I remembered, simultaneously, getting miffed with her that day for having spilled ketchup all over her shirt.

I turned to look at the poised young woman next to me and wondered how much I missed on this journey from worry—how I thought we should buy stock in VELCRO® because she was never going to learn to tie her shoes. How we could never go out to eat without her smearing some food substance all over her front. How many lunch boxes and coats we'd go through each school year for her having lost so many. How many reminders fell on deaf ears about putting her homework in some semblance of order. Days after months after years scrolled through my memory, and I just shook my head, smiling, because this particular road trip came the day after we received the admissions letter from her first choice of college.

How in the world did we get here?

At church the next day, we were asked to think of one thing requiring amends and one thing requiring thanks. What came to mind immediately is how quickly I can believe that my own will and wiliness have gotten us this far, that somehow my millions of admonitions about remembering homework and forgetting coats got her into college. My pride routinely makes me forget how much He has done.

After the service, I got to talk with one of our pastors, sharing Emma's good news and wondering aloud at the grace that brought us this far; seen from the long view, it is stunning and humbling. This pastor has walked a long and littered path with me over 15 years, so she knows both the ugliness and the healing that have taken place. But she also reminded me of the Scripture below—how all of mankind forgets, and how we're told again and again not to.

At the end of this particular journey, I stop to remember, and ask you to do the same—where we have been and where we are going. Who is with us and who is for us. How we have been, and will be, fed and led and blessed, all by the One who is faithful.

On this road, *remember*.

As you look at your children today, what worries do you recall that never came to pass?

Who and what helped you along to the place you're at today?

ONE VERSE FOR THOUGHT:
He led you through the vast and dreadful wilderness, that thirsty and waterless land, with its venomous snakes and scorpions. He brought you water out of hard rock. He gave you manna to eat in the wilderness, something your ancestors had never known, to humble and test you so that in the end it might go well with you. You may say to yourself, "My power and the strength of my hands have produced this wealth for me." But remember the Lord your God, for it is he who gives you the ability to produce wealth, and so confirms his covenant, which he swore to your ancestors, as it is today. **–Deuteronomy 8:15-18, NIV**

afterword:
one hard goodbye

When my daughter got her early acceptance to college, I was talking with God about how grateful I was—that we made it this far, that she had this awesome opportunity, that it would be such a good thing. I was just so happy for her. Then I heard Him ask quietly, "Would you let me bless you, too?"

As I sat in the possibility of something new and different for me after Em leaves, I received a paradox: It was time for me to leave, too—back to the Midwest, to the town in which I was raised. I sat with this and prayed and waited, and I received some pointed, poignant Scripture references. Finally, after much prayer and consideration, I said yes, I'll go...into whatever lies ahead.

I've experienced this once before in my life, getting the "time to leave" message in the same crazy way—when I was in a good situation and generally content, as I have been as of late. The last time it happened, it quickly resulted in the crazy dream that became Eve's Daughters. Now, I have no idea what's on the horizon; it seems He and I are on a "need to know" basis, and I have no need to know at this particular juncture. I'm sure it will come.

I will be grateful to be two states away from my girl versus seven, able to see her more often in a place that will always feel like home. But as for the rest—finding work, restoring friendships, uncovering whatever He has for me next—I will be starting over again.

The decision to end Eve's Daughters was wrenching and emotional, but we as a Board determined it was the right thing to do at the right time. We finish knowing we worked hard and long to provide a true community for the single moms and kids in our midst. We may never know what ripples spread from our existence these past nine years. Maybe we don't need to. At that hard meeting, one of our original Board members, Shelley, reminded us of the story about the boy who was walking a beach littered with stranded starfish, tossing them back into the ocean and knowing he couldn't save them all but he could make a difference to a few.

Maybe that's what we were able to do as well.

While my time in Oregon has been tough in many ways (the hard marriage, the harder divorce, the single motherhood, and the cleaning up of my own debris), it's also been refining. For that, I'm incredibly grateful. I'm going back to a place I'm sure has changed significantly but, then again, so have I. Like Jacob in the book of Genesis, I've wrestled with God the past two-plus decades and have my own limp to show for it, but I'll bet all my flailing will be put to good use at my next stop.

And yet…this will be one hard goodbye. I leave treasured friends who've literally transformed my life. I leave a Board that walked Cathy and I through a thousand discussions and decisions. I leave a church family who welcomed me back into the fold after twenty-plus years of wandering. I leave generous clients, work colleagues, and neighbors I adore. And I leave the women of Eve's Daughters who have impacted me far more than I've impacted them. Every one, unforgettable.

It kind of feels like I'll be losing two babies this year—one to college and one to posterity—but it has been an honor and a privilege to walk with them both. I feel as blessed by you, dear readers, and am grateful you brought the essence of Eve's Daughters into your lives. Thank you.

acknowledgements

Many thanks to my early draft reviewers, including Cathy Brewer, Patricia Dahlberg, Bonnie Gorshe, Kathy Holmquist, Anne Keddington, Colin and Kathy Kuskie, Elaine Marin, Meghan Mowry, Pat O'Connor, Alan Pelzner and Sharon Rose, along with much gratitude to proofreader Sarah Bokich.

Much appreciation to authors Kathy Vick and Steve Wiens for permission to use their materials herein.

Grateful to Machele Brass for her expert assistance in designing this volume.

Hugs and kisses to Dorothy, Eric and Kimberly Sjoblom for their continuous support.

Deep thankfulness to our amazing Eve's Daughters Board (Shelley Hutchinson, Donna Larson and Deb Stewart) and the awesome Annie Salness for getting us started all those years ago.

Humbly indebted to all the single moms who were generous enough to share their stories herein.

And to my Emma: Beyond grateful for who you've been, who you are and who you're becoming. Thank you for rocking my world.

on building your own
single mom community

We've had so many calls, emails and requests over the years about starting something like Eve's Daughters in other areas of the country. We believe the need for such community is huge, but the investment to create it doesn't have to be. What Cathy and I were able to do with our nonprofit wasn't rocket science, but rather was a simple commitment to facilitating fellowship and eliminating isolation. That was the primary goal. Then, we asked ourselves what else our moms could use—mentors, emergency funding, connections to local resources, small group support, book studies—and added those facets to the mix as the years went on.

Maybe there's a small group of single moms in your neighborhood, church, synagogue or school district, and you're ready to build your own supportive community. Yes! Go forth and build!! Here are some simple ideas to get you started on your way…keeping in mind you can tailor everything to suit your specific wants and needs.

Create a Meetup group (www.meetup.com)
for single moms in your area
Research and plan free and fun family-friendly outings to expand your single mom social circle.

Organize a monthly potluck dinner
There's something about sharing a meal together that builds community like nothing else. Request a meeting room at your local house of worship, library or community center, bring the kids and start getting to know other single moms and their children. Then, keep in touch virtually in between get-togethers.

START A PRIVATE FACEBOOK PAGE TO SHARE NEWS, NEEDS AND WANTS

If you need to get rid of your kid's size 3T clothes, and someone else has some 4Ts to get rid of, you're golden. Share what you have and what you need, and develop an online community to help augment your face-to-face gatherings.

DEVELOP A SMALL GROUP FOR SUPPORT AND STUDY

If you find a few single moms with whom you've really connected, go deeper with a regular group meeting to share what's happening in each other's lives, study and discuss a book together or simply share day-to-day life with each other.

In the end, you'll find a whole continuum of single parents—some with newborns, some with teens—who are happy to share what they need and what they've learned..and your family will be better for having known them.

We have been really blessed to see so many of our community's kids grow strong alongside their amazing moms; in this manner, Eve's Daughters was truly a successful experiment in how to bring strangers together and change them into friends. Many of our moms and kids have investigated shared housing, go on vacations together, share resources and so much more. Where moms once were totally alone, there is now a family... and that's been the most amazing transformation.

To share your thoughts or get additional information, email karen@karensjoblom.com. I look forward to hearing all the ways you're creating a single mom community in your neighborhood!

Made in the USA
San Bernardino, CA
06 April 2016

filling you up, two pages at a time

If you've ever wondered how you got to this place, what you need to make it through, whether the loneliness will subside, and if the money (and your energy) will hold out until your kids are raised, you'll find your story on these pages…required reading for every single mom.

One traces the full-circle journey of solo parenting, capturing both the ordinary and extraordinary and proving you really only need a single point of connection to keep going—even on your hardest days. Designed to be read on-the-fly, these short stories meet you where you're at with all the black humor, occasional despair, and surprising joy inherent in raising children alone. They celebrate the sustenance provided by connections to God and each other, and invite women to take courage from hard endings that give way to wobbly, promising beginnings. With wisdom on building community, embracing our imperfections, forgiving ourselves and others, and staggering triumphantly to the other side of great loss, One refills and refreshes single moms up to their elbows in life and living.

Karen Sjoblom is a writer and the co-founder of Eve's Daughters, a nonprofit for single moms outside of Portland, Oregon. A long-time solo parent, Karen engages and encourages women toward community, faith, and a deeper appreciation of the glorious chaos that is single mothering. She is the grateful mom of Emma and BeBe the Gassy Wonder Dog.

ISBN 9781530791705

90000

9 781530 791705